Artificial Intelligence–Based Student Activity Monitoring for Suicide Risk

Considerations for K–12 Schools, Caregivers, Government, and Technology Developers

LYNSAY AYER, BENJAMIN BOUDREAUX,
JESSICA WELBURN PAIGE, PIERRCE HOLMES,
TARA LAILA BLAGG, SAPNA J. MENDON-PLASEK

For more information on this publication, visit **www.rand.org/t/RRA2910-1**.

About RAND

The RAND Corporation is a research organization that develops solutions to public policy challenges to help make communities throughout the world safer and more secure, healthier and more prosperous. RAND is nonprofit, nonpartisan, and committed to the public interest. To learn more about RAND, visit www.rand.org.

Research Integrity

Our mission to help improve policy and decisionmaking through research and analysis is enabled through our core values of quality and objectivity and our unwavering commitment to the highest level of integrity and ethical behavior. To help ensure our research and analysis are rigorous, objective, and nonpartisan, we subject our research publications to a robust and exacting quality-assurance process; avoid both the appearance and reality of financial and other conflicts of interest through staff training, project screening, and a policy of mandatory disclosure; and pursue transparency in our research engagements through our commitment to the open publication of our research findings and recommendations, disclosure of the source of funding of published research, and policies to ensure intellectual independence. For more information, visit www.rand.org/about/research-integrity.

RAND's publications do not necessarily reflect the opinions of its research clients and sponsors.

Published by the RAND Corporation, Santa Monica, Calif.
© 2023 RAND Corporation
RAND® is a registered trademark.

Library of Congress Cataloging-in-Publication Data is available for this publication.
ISBN: 978-1-9774-1263-8

Cover composite image: Matty Symons/Adobe Stock and TechSolution/Adobe Stock

Limited Print and Electronic Distribution Rights

About This Report

Schools are increasingly relying on artificial intelligence (AI) technology to assist with a variety of tasks, including identifying students who are at risk for suicide. Specifically, schools use software that is loaded on school-issued devices to monitor students' digital activity (e.g., Google search terms). This software applies proprietary algorithms and alerts school staff when a student's activity suggests suicide risk. These programs have been the subject of controversy, but there is scant research on how they are used and their potential risks and benefits. The main goal of this report is to document how AI-based suicide risk monitoring is being implemented in schools and how it is affecting communities. Using this information, we offer recommendations for schools, caregivers, policymakers, and technology developers.

RAND Education and Labor

This study was undertaken by RAND Education and Labor, a division of the RAND Corporation that conducts research on early childhood through postsecondary education programs, workforce development, and programs and policies affecting workers, entrepreneurship, and financial literacy and decisionmaking.

More information about RAND can be found at www.rand.org. Questions about this report should be directed to Lynsay_Ayer@rand.org, and questions about RAND Education and Labor should be directed to educationandlabor@rand.org.

Funding

Funding for this research was provided by gifts from RAND supporters and income from operations.

Acknowledgments

We are grateful for the feedback and guidance provided by many colleagues as we developed the study concept and designed our research procedures, including Lisa Jaycox and Nancy Staudt of RAND. We are also grateful to our colleagues who provided a thorough review of and feedback on drafts of this report, namely Elizabeth Steiner of RAND and Elizabeth Laird of the Center for Democracy and Technology.

Summary

Suicide is the second leading cause of death among youth age ten to 19. Youth suicide is a rapidly growing phenomenon; rates increased by 70 percent between 2009 and 2019 (Agency for Healthcare Research and Quality, 2022; Centers for Disease Control and Prevention, 2021). Youth hospital visits for mental health reasons, including suicide, significantly increased during the first two years of the coronavirus disease 2019 (COVID-19) pandemic (Overhage et al., 2023).

The increase in youth suicide risk since 2009 coincides with a shortage of youth mental health professionals. One study found that mental health workforce shortages, which occur most often in rural areas and low-income communities, were significantly correlated with increased suicide rates in five- to 19-year-olds (Hoffmann et al., 2023).

Research suggests that evidence-based suicide prevention programming in schools has the potential to help fill gaps in youth mental health care (Singer, Erbacher, and Rosen, 2019). Schools are on the front line of addressing youth mental health and suicide concerns (Ayer and Colpe, 2022). However, many U.S. schools are facing other challenges, including ongoing pandemic recovery efforts, teacher burnout, and teacher shortages (Doan et al., 2023; Nguyen, Lam, and Bruno, 2022; Steiner et al., 2022).

In response to the widespread youth mental health crisis, some kindergarten through 12th grade (K–12) schools have begun employing artificial intelligence (AI)-based tools to help identify students at risk for suicide and self-harm. The adoption of AI and other types of educational technology (EdTech) to partially address student mental health needs has been a natural forward step for many schools during the transition to remote education during the COVID-19 pandemic. However, there is limited understanding about how such programs work, how they are implemented by schools, and how they may benefit or harm students and their families (Bason, 2021; Laird et al., 2022; Madhusudan, 2021; Office of Senator Elizabeth Warren, 2022; Patterson, 2021; Shinde, 2021).

To assist policymakers, school districts, school leaders, and others in making decisions regarding the use of these tools, this report addresses these knowledge gaps by providing a preliminary examination of how AI-based suicide risk monitoring programs are implemented in K–12 schools, how stakeholders perceive the effects that the programs are having on students, and the potential benefits and risks of such tools. Using this analysis, we also offer recommendations for school and district leaders; state, federal, and local policymakers; and technology developers to consider as they move forward in maximizing the intended benefits and mitigating the possible risks of AI-based suicide risk monitoring programs.

Key Findings

Our analysis produced the following key findings:

- Interviews with school staff, EdTech company representatives, health care professionals, and advocacy group staff and members suggest that AI-based suicide risk monitoring tools can help identify K–12 students who are at risk for suicide and provide reassurance for school staff and caregivers.
- Prior research shows that AI-based suicide risk prediction algorithms—and, by extension, student activity monitoring in schools—can compromise student privacy and perpetuate existing inequalities.
- There is a need for data that show how accurately AI-based algorithms can detect a student's risk of suicide and whether the use of these tools improves student mental health.
- K–12 schools and their broader communities are often not sufficiently resourced to respond to youth mental health challenges, even with the use of AI-based suicide risk monitoring.
- Key community members—including pediatric providers, mental health counselors, and caregivers—play important roles in the implementation of these tools, but community members might be unaware of how the tools are used by K–12 schools to detect student suicide risk.

Contents

APPENDIXES

Figure and Table

Figure

Table

CHAPTER 1

Introduction

Suicide is the second leading cause of death among youth age ten to 19. Youth suicide is a rapidly growing phenomenon; rates increased by 70 percent between 2009 and 2019 (Agency for Healthcare Research and Quality, 2022; Centers for Disease Control and Prevention, 2021). Youth hospital visits for mental health reasons, including suicide, significantly increased during the first two years of the coronavirus disease 2019 (COVID-19) pandemic (Overhage et al., 2023).

The increase in youth suicide risk since 2009 coincides with a shortage of youth mental health professionals. One study found that mental health workforce shortages, which occur most often in rural areas and low-income communities, were significantly correlated with increased suicide rates in five- to 19-year-olds (Hoffmann et al., 2023).

Research suggests that evidence-based suicide prevention programming in schools has the potential to help fill gaps in youth mental health care (Singer, Erbacher, and Rosen, 2019). Schools are on the front line of addressing youth mental health and suicide concerns (Ayer and Colpe, 2022). However, many U.S. schools are facing other challenges, including ongoing pandemic recovery efforts, teacher burnout, and teacher shortages (Doan et al., 2023; Nguyen, Lam, and Bruno, 2022; Steiner et al., 2022).

In response to the widespread youth mental health crisis, some kindergarten through 12th grade (K–12) schools have begun employing tools that use artificial intelligence (AI) to help identify students at risk for suicide and self-harm. The adoption of AI and other types of educational technology (EdTech) to partially address student mental health needs has been a natural forward step for many schools during the transition to remote education during the COVID-19 pandemic. However, there is limited understanding about how such tools work, how they are implemented by schools, and how these tools might benefit or harm students and their families (Bason, 2021; Laird et al., 2022; Madhusudan, 2021; Office of Senator Elizabeth Warren, 2022; Patterson, 2021; Shinde, 2021).

To assist policymakers, school districts, school leaders, and others in making decisions regarding the use of these tools, this report addresses these knowledge gaps by providing a preliminary examination of how AI-based suicide risk monitoring programs are implemented in K–12 schools, how stakeholders perceive the effects that the programs are having on students, and the potential benefits and risks of such tools. Using this analysis, we also offer recommendations for school and district leaders; state, federal, and local policymakers; and technology developers to consider as they move forward in maximizing the intended benefits and mitigating the possible risks of AI-based suicide risk monitoring programs.

Background

In recent years, EdTech companies, including GoGuardian, Bark for Schools, Securly, and Gaggle, have developed AI-based algorithms to detect risk for suicide, self-harm, and harm to others through students' digital activity.[1] Schools contract with these companies to monitor student activity on school-owned devices and accounts. If the algorithm identifies potentially risky student activities, the system alerts adults to intervene; for instance, a school staff member or the police would be contacted to respond to the alert. In this report, we use the term *AI-based suicide risk monitoring* to refer to these tools that monitor student's activity on school-issued devices and accounts to identify suicidal ideation and risk of self-harm, including suicide attempts.

AI-based suicide risk monitoring is implemented with the best of intentions; schools want a way to identify students who are at risk for suicide. Some studies suggest that these programs might help identify suicide risk factors and potentially save lives (Byars et al., 2020; Sumner et al., 2021).

---

[1] Many of these companies also offer other services, such as internet content filtering to prevent access to certain websites and classroom management tools. However, we did not evaluate these additional services because this report focuses on how these AI products are designed to detect risk for suicide or self-harm.

For example, a student considering suicide might not share their thoughts or feelings with anyone who can intervene. Their online activity could be the only outward or observable indication that the student is at risk. Furthermore, schools might lack the resources to conduct systematic, universal suicide risk screening and safety assessments, which means that passive monitoring of students' online activity to look for indicators of suicidal thoughts, plans, or behaviors can be seen as a cost-effective way to reduce student suicide risk.

However, as with any tool used for monitoring, there are potential risks. In the case of AI-based student monitoring, potential risks relate to privacy violations and other unintended harms, particularly for marginalized communities (Laird et al., 2022). Specifically, there is a risk that these tools could jeopardize students' privacy and perpetuate or exacerbate existing inequities. Research has shown that there is significant potential for bias in AI-based algorithms, which might negatively affect already-marginalized communities, such as lesbian, gay, bisexual, transgender, queer, or questioning (LGBTQ+) people; racial or ethnic minority groups; and people with disabilities (Ferrer et al., 2021). This bias occurs in part because AI models are built on data that reflect historical inequities. For example, research suggests that the online language typically used by people of color is more likely to be deemed risky or harmful than the language typically used by White people; as a result, alerts based on online language could have a disparate impact on students of color (Chung, 2019; Gellman and Adler-Bell, 2017). Moreover, students from lower socioeconomic groups might be more likely to use school-issued devices than personally owned devices (Vogels, 2021). Thus, their computer activity is more likely to be monitored, and they are more likely to be the subject of AI-generated alerts for risky behavior that result in interactions with law enforcement or otherwise result in disciplinary action by their school or caregivers.

These potential risks have been discussed. Congressional inquiries, for example, have probed AI-based student suicide risk monitoring companies for more information on how they monitor K–12 students and address such issues as data privacy (Office of Senator Elizabeth Warren, 2022). However, no research to date has comprehensively examined how these programs affect youth suicide prevention or assessed their risks and benefits.

Research Questions, Methods, and Limitations

As stated, there is only scant evidence related to the outcomes of these programs and to their benefits and risks. To address the need for analyses, we first document how AI-based suicide risk monitoring is being implemented in K–12 schools. We then examine how some stakeholders believe it is affecting students. Using this analysis, we then offer recommendations for schools, policymakers, and technology developers who play key roles in the implementation of these tools.

Our specific research questions consist of the following:

- What has existing research found about how accurately AI-based suicide risk monitoring identifies youth who are at risk for suicide?
- How is AI-based suicide risk monitoring being used in K–12 schools to detect and prevent youth suicide risk and self-harm?
- What is the perceived impact of these programs on students, what are their potential risks, and how can benefits be realized while mitigating risks?
- What are the best practices and recommendations for schools, caregivers, technology developers, and policymakers seeking to use these technologies in K–12 schools while preventing potential harms?

Data and Methods

Data for this analysis were collected from the following three sources:

- **peer-reviewed literature** on how technology is being used to identify suicide risk
- **gray literature,** such as EdTech company documents
- **semistructured interviews** with school staff, EdTech company representatives, health care professionals, and members of advocacy groups (see Appendix C for full list of respondents).

A detailed description of our study methods is provided in the appendixes. In brief, we reviewed 132 research studies on the use of technology to prevent suicide in school-aged youth. We also conducted 22 semistructured interviews with a convenience sample of respondents from schools, EdTech companies, health care providers, and advocacy groups to collect qualitative data on implementation and impact. Interviews were approximately 60 minutes long and conducted remotely (e.g., via Zoom.gov).

All interviews were guided by a semistructured interview protocol covering a variety of topics, including the interviewee's job, position, and background; experience and familiarity with the AI-based tools; views of the tools (including benefits, risks, advantages, and disadvantages); how these tools do or do not complement other school-based suicide prevention programs; best practices and lessons learned in using the tools; and recommendations for policymakers, schools, and technology companies. The full interview protocols and a list of respondents are provided in Appendixes B and C.

Limitations

This report focuses on how AI-based suicide risk monitoring programs are used in schools and their risks and benefits from the perspectives of our interview respondents. Before discussing our findings, it is important to consider the report's limitations. These limitations fall into four overall areas.

First, it is important to note that we approached the key research questions from a high-level view; we did not, for example, compare the implementation of these programs within and between schools and districts or communities. We note that we originally planned to use a deep-dive approach that examined one large school district, but this became infeasible after high-level district leaders declined to allow our data collection out of concern that the topic and potential findings could cause unwanted criticism or controversy. The controversial nature of the research is another notable challenge because it could lead to reluctance to share data or information that might become subject to public discussion and scrutiny.

Second, although our interviews did capture multiple perspectives and experiences, this was a small convenience sample. Therefore, the views of our study participants likely do not represent the views of all individuals in these groups. We were only able to interview seven school staff members (i.e., not a representative sample). Interview data from students who have had direct experiences with these programs were not available. Consequently, student perspectives are missing from this report.

Third, there are biases inherent to interview data that we are not able to quantify but which are likely to be present in this report, as is the case for all studies that use this type of data. We were not able to verify participants' responses for accuracy, and participants might have been motivated to give socially desirable responses.

Finally, this report did not include a comprehensive legal review and analysis of the relevant state, local, and federal policies that could be relevant to whether and how these programs are used in schools.

How This Report Is Organized

In Chapter 2, we summarize the existing research on known risk factors for youth suicide and how technology has been used to identify suicide risk among youth. Chapter 3 offers specific details on how AI-based suicide risk monitoring is being used in schools and an analysis of documents from several major companies. We then describe our interview respondents' perceived benefits and risks of AI-based suicide risk monitoring in Chapter 4. Finally, in Chapter 5, we present key findings and recommendations for schools, policymakers, and EdTech companies.

This analysis is supported by three appendixes. Appendix A offers detailed description of our interview methods. The full interview protocols are provided in Appendix B. Appendix C presents the full list of respondents who participated in our interviews (we use pseudonyms to preserve confidentiality).

CHAPTER 2

Youth Suicide and Artificial-Intelligence–Based Risk Detection

In this chapter, we address our first research question: What has existing research found about how accurately AI-based suicide risk monitoring identifies youth who are at risk for suicide? To do so, we reviewed the research literature on youth suicide risk factors and how AI-based algorithms have been used to identify or predict suicide risk.

Risk Factors for Youth Suicide

We begin our summary of the research literature by focusing on the evidence for various suicide risk factors that EdTech companies might use as key indicators in their suicide risk prediction algorithms (Sumner et al., 2021). We use the word *might* because we were not able to obtain information from the EdTech companies about the specific data and indicators that are used in their algorithms or how heavily each indicator is weighted. However, limited evidence does suggest that these risk factors (as indicated or measured by students' online activity) could be important pieces of the algorithms that ultimately determine whether the student might be at risk for suicide (McCarthy et al., 2021; Sumner et al., 2021).

Race, Ethnicity, Sexual Orientation, Sex, and Gender Identity

Although suicide is an increasing public health concern for all school-age youth, risk varies by race, gender, and sexual orientation. Suicide death rates among youth are highest for Native American and Alaskan Native males (Bridge et al., 2023). Suicide attempts and suicidal ideation rates are higher and have increased more rapidly in years for youth who identify as female; LGBTQ+; or Black, Hispanic, or Native American (Centers for Disease Control and Prevention, 2022). For example, the 2021 Youth Risk Behavior Survey found that 13 percent of female high school students reported attempting suicide within the past year, compared with 7 percent of male students. Among students identifying as LGBTQ+, this number was 22 percent, compared with 6 percent of heterosexual students (Centers for Disease Control and Prevention, 2022). Findings from the 2015 U.S. Transgender Survey indicated that more than 40 percent of transgender individuals reported attempting suicide during their youth and adolescence (Austin et al., 2022).

Mental Health, Adverse Experiences, and Social Media Use

Mental health disorders are common among youth who experience suicidal thoughts and behaviors. For example, in up to 65 percent of youth suicide cases, the youth experienced depression; co-occurring mental health problems, including substance use, further increase suicide risk (Bilsen, 2018). Other risk factors include a history of abuse or adverse childhood experience, bullying. availability of lethal means (e.g., firearms), and social stress or isolation (Bilsen, 2018). The convergence of these risk factors with the COVID-19 pandemic might have driven the growing rate of youth suicide (Ridout et al., 2021; Samji et al., 2022).

Evidence also suggests that social media could be contributing to the increase in youth suicide, especially among youth who are already vulnerable, such as youth with preexisting mental health conditions (U.S. Surgeon General, 2023). One study of a cohort of 10,904 14-year-olds found that greater social media usage is associated with online harassment, poor sleep, low self-esteem, low body image, and depression (Kelly et al., 2018). Social media usage and its associated negative mental health and harassment consequences were found to be higher among girls than among boys (Kelly et al., 2018).

Using Artificial Intelligence to Identify Individuals at Risk for Suicide

A critical and unanswered question is whether the algorithms meant to detect student suicide risk are accurately detecting that risk. In this case, *accuracy* is the extent to which the tool is maximizing detection of *true positives*—youth flagged as at risk who truly were at risk—while minimizing *false positives*—youth flagged as at risk who were not at risk—and *false negatives*—youth at risk who were not flagged as at risk. The accuracy of these tools is difficult to determine in practice, however, because assessment requires systematic collection of information on the actual, real-time suicide risk and outcomes of youth who both were and were not flagged as at risk for suicide.

One study, along with letters from the four major EdTech companies in response to a congressional inquiry, suggests that these algorithms can help identify suicide risk factors in many youth (Sumner et al., 2021; Bason, 2021; Madhusudan, 2021; Patterson, 2021; Shinde, 2021). For example, these sources suggest that AI systems can identify statistical patterns in health, socioeconomic, or computer activities (e.g., chat, social media posts, search activity) that are often correlated with suicidal ideation or self-harm behavior. However, AI systems have not been measured for their capacity to predict specific instances of suicidal ideation or self-harm behavior. It is important to note that no studies have examined the accuracy—including the potential for false positives or negatives—of the specific AI-based suicide risk monitoring used in schools that is the focus of this report. Therefore, we focused the rest of our review on studies of suicide risk identification or prediction algorithms that use other types of data (e.g., health records data) because they represent the best available evidence.

It is also important to note that many non-AI-driven youth suicide risk screening and assessment tools already exist and are used in K–12 schools. Our literature review does not cover those tools or the data on their reliability, validity, sensitivity, and specificity, but we recommend that interested readers refer to published reviews that can help inform the selection of valid screening tools and their implementation in school settings (Cwik, O'Keefe, and Haroz, 2020; Singer, Erbacher, and Rosen, 2019).

Medical and Health Records Data Might Be Useful for Artificial-Intelligence–Based Suicide Risk Identification

The literature suggests that AI is most effective at detecting suicide risk when data used to supply models were mainly from medical sources, such as electronic health records data (Lejeune et al., 2022). One child suicide risk prediction algorithm studying 5,885 children age nine to 11 used socio-demographic, physical health, social-environmental, neuroimaging, genetic, and clinical psychiatric variables from electronic health records to predict suicide attempts and ideation. Clinical psychological variables, such as past suicide attempts and history of mental health issues, were the strongest predictors, and the algorithm differentiated the suicidal children from the nonsuicidal control group 70 percent of the time (van Velzen et al., 2022).

Medical data gathered from clinical screening tools and health questionnaires have also proven useful for algorithms that attempt to identify adolescent and youth suicide risk (King et al., 2021; van Vuuren et al., 2021; Zheng et al., 2022). One screening tool that measures suicidal ideation and rumination, nonsuicidal self-injury, depression, homicidal ideation, anxiety, posttraumatic stress disorder, social adjustment, sleep amounts, aggression, and substance use was able to predict adolescents' risk for suicide attempt (King et al., 2021). Another model that uses data gathered from a health questionnaire regarding lifestyle behaviors, physical and mental health, and environmental safety was able to predict middle school students' suicidal ideations (van Vuuren et al., 2021).

It is important to note that these suicide risk prediction algorithms that are driven by health records data are primarily used by health systems to identify *groups* of patients who might benefit from safety planning or increased monitoring rather than to detect *individual* mental health emergencies that require immediate responses (McCarthy et al., 2021).

There Is Limited Evidence for Accuracy of Online Activity Data Detecting Suicide Risk

The AI-based programs used by schools that are the subject of this report do not use medical or health records data. Rather, their algorithms rely on data from students' online activity (e.g., Google search terms) to determine suicide risk. Some studies have shown that data collected from social sources have the potential to correctly identify emotions and behaviors that have been shown to be predictors of suicide risk (D'Hotman and Loh, 2020). Several algorithms have used social media posts, such as posts from Twitter and Reddit, to identify such suicide risk factors as cyberbullying victimization (96 percent accuracy [Bharti et al., 2022]) and depression (73 percent accuracy [De Choudhury et al., 2021]) in adolescents, although these algorithms have not identified suicidal thoughts and behaviors themselves. One evaluation of an algorithm that is intended to identify suicidal thoughts expressed on social media platforms found that classifiers were able to correctly identify emotions but did not assess whether the identified emotions related to suicidal thoughts or behaviors (Shree and Chudhey, 2021).

Visual and auditory data that might be collected from cameras and microphones on school-issued devices have also been discussed as one way to identify suicide risk factors in adolescents (Barua et al., 2022; Zhang et al., 2022). One study evaluated the association between a set of data types (including texts, images, and video data that indicated cyberbullying, drug-related content, hate speech, sexual content, profanity, self-harm, violence, and depression) and the risk of youth being flagged for an imminent suicide alert. The study found that all risk factor data except hate speech were associated with a higher probability of a youth being flagged for an imminent suicide risk alert (Sumner et al., 2021). Depression-related content had the largest association with imminent suicide risk alerts, and the probability of an alert increased with each additional risk factor (Sumner et al., 2021). However, this study did not assess whether the suicide risk alerts were accurate (i.e., whether the student was in fact thinking about suicide or engaging in self-harm). Other apps, such as mental health chatbots and apps that measure depression and suicide risk through user mobility and cell phone usage, are in use and development. However, there is limited evidence that these apps can correctly identify suicide risk (Barry, 2022).

Suicide Risk Identification or Prediction Algorithms Can Be Biased

Although there is still limited research examining bias in AI-based suicide risk monitoring software programs used in schools, research on the use of AI in other areas highlights the possibility for bias in algorithms—even if it is unintended (Ferrer et al., 2021; Mehrabi et al., 2021). Mehrabi et al. (2021) detailed several potential sources of algorithmic bias. These sources include

- *data-to-algorithm bias*: statistical biases in the data that feed the algorithm
- *algorithm-to user-bias*: bias in user behavior that develops from using the algorithm
- *user-to-data bias*: biases among users of programs, tools and other platforms that are used to generate data that subsequently feeds algorithms.

The authors of those sources argued that these types of bias can have a significant impact on machine learning data. For example, AI tools might perpetuate discrimination against people of color or women because they draw on existing, biased data.

As discussed previously in this report, a growing body of research provides additional evidence that bias in machine learning models can be significant. For example, Kapur (2021) argued that AI algorithms used to make medical diagnoses may discriminate against patients of color by either misdiagnosing them or failing to diagnose them at all (Kapur, 2021). This discrimination can occur because the algorithms themselves are developed using data that reflect historical inequalities. Blodgett and O'Connor (2017) explored the potential for racial differences in natural language processing, another example of potential AI bias. Using Twitter posts, they found that natural language processing was less effective at analyzing language used by women and people of color than language used by men and White people.

Overall, more research is needed to add to the limited literature on the ability of AI to correctly detect suicide risk in at-risk youth from diverse backgrounds (Bernert et al., 2020). Several studies point to the need for models that are sensitive to differing communities' norms and health care usage to accurately predict suicidality and prevent algorithmic biases (Walsh et al., 2020). For example, one study found that a suicide risk prediction model that utilizes health records data—including comorbidities, diagnoses, prior mental health encounters, and a depression screening tool—was significantly more accurate for White, Hispanic, and Asian patients than for Black and Native American or Alaskan Native patients (Coley et al., 2021).

Suicide risk prediction algorithms using social data can also be prone to algorithmic bias, as shown by studies that have found that algorithms perform poorly when utilizing social media data, facial imagery, and speech samples collected from racial and ethnic minority groups compared with data collected from White groups (Blodgett and O'Connor, 2017; Hitczenko et al., 2022). However, algorithms for suicide risk prediction that have been tested and developed specifically for use within at-risk subgroups, such as one algorithm tested among Alaskan Native populations (Shaw et al., 2022) and another developed for use among Native American communities (Haroz et al., 2020), have had more promising results.

Law and Policy Regarding Artificial-Intelligence–Based Suicide Risk Monitoring in Schools

Laws and policies related to the use of AI generally and in schools specifically are actively being reviewed and revised at the federal, state, and local levels. A full legal review is beyond the scope of this project; however, research suggests that there are gaps in law and policy. Although there are several laws regarding the protection of student data and health data more generally, these laws do not apply to online activity monitoring conducted to identify suicide risk among students. For example, the Family Educational Rights and Privacy Act (FERPA) protects the privacy of students' educational records (such as grades and transcripts) by preventing schools or teachers from disclosing students' records while allowing caregivers access to those records to review or correct them (U.S. Department of Education, 2021). However, the information from computer activity on school-issued devices or accounts is not usually considered an education record and is thus not subject to FERPA's protections (U.S. Department of Education, undated). Similarly, the Health Information Portability and Accountability Act (HIPAA) protects specific health information collected by covered entities but does not protect the collection of use of computer activity by students, and EdTech companies are not considered "covered entities" (U.S. Department of Health and Human Services, undated). Beyond these laws, there is no federal data privacy law that protects the privacy of information collected by these programs. This lack of protection suggests that there is a substantial legal gap for students.

There is uncertainty about how other laws apply to student monitoring tools. For instance, the Children's Internet Protection Act (CIPA) seeks to protect students from accessing obscene or harmful activity online. One provision of CIPA requires that schools' "Internet safety policies must include monitoring the online activities of minors" (Federal Communications Commission, 2019). According to some reports, AI-based online activity monitoring to detect suicide risk might be seen as fostering compliance with this provision (Hankerson et al., 2021). However, some U.S. senators have argued that this interpretation "goes well beyond the purpose of the law" (Office of Senator Elizabeth Warren, 2022).

It is also unclear how recent executive branch policy documents pertaining to AI apply to these programs. The White House report *Blueprint for an AI Bill of Rights* offers several principles for the design, deployment, and use of AI across social institutions, including principles that pertain to privacy, equity, and notice and explanation regarding the use of AI products (White House, 2022). *Blueprint for an AI Bill of Rights* also articulates several references to the role of AI in schools, such as "continuous surveillance and monitoring should not be used in education . . . where the use of such surveillance technologies is likely to limit rights, opportunities, or access" and "automated systems with an intended use within sensitive domains, including . . . education, and health, should additionally be tailored to the purpose, [and] provide meaningful access for oversight" (White House, 2022, pp. 6, 46). However, it is not clear how these efforts to promote privacy, equity, and accountability apply to AI-based suicide risk monitoring. Similarly, the Department of Education's report on the use of AI in schools does not discuss the use of student online activity monitoring software or its possible risks of violating privacy and civil liberties (U.S. Department of Education, 2023).

Some independent efforts have been made to vet the privacy policies of EdTech companies. For example, the Future of Privacy Forum and the Software & Information Industry Association created the Student Privacy Pledge 2020 (Future of Privacy Forum and the Software & Information Industry Association, undated-a), which seeks to vet the privacy efforts of independent EdTech companies. Gaggle, GoGuardian, and Securly have all voluntarily committed to the pledge. To be listed as signatories, companies must apply and have their privacy policies assessed by Student Privacy Pledge leadership. The pledge includes several key commitments from companies regarding use of student data, including:

- We will not knowingly retain Student PII [personally identifiable information] beyond the time period required to support the authorized educational/school purposes, or as authorized by the parent/student.
- We will collect, use, share, and retain Student PII only for purposes for which we were authorized by the educational institution/agency, teacher or the parent/student.
- We will disclose clearly in contracts or privacy policies, including in a manner easy for institutions and parents to find and understand, what types of Student PII we collect, if any, and the purposes for which the information we maintain is used or shared with third parties. (Future of Privacy Forum and the Software & Information Industry Association, undated-a)

The pledge emphasizes that, by signing, companies have made a public statement about their privacy policies, and violations may be enforced by the Federal Trade Commission (FTC). The pledge also notes its own limitations:

The Pledge is limited in scope to the commitments it outlines. The Pledge is not intended to be a comprehensive privacy policy nor to be inclusive of all the many requirements needed to comply with applicable federal and state laws. That said, most Signatories have taken the Pledge because they wish to be thoughtful and conscientious about privacy and are therefore likely to have done a thorough analysis of the requirements at all levels and attempted to comply. (Future of Privacy Forum and the Software & Information Industry Association, undated-b)

Common Sense—a nonprofit company that examines and evaluates media and technology issues affecting children—also provides independent assessments of some EdTech companies' privacy policies (Common Sense, undated-a). Its evaluation system assesses companies on several privacy dimensions—such as data collection, data security, and data sharing; the lower the score on a scale from 0 percent to 100 percent, the lower the rating (Common Sense, undated-b). Companies are then given comprehensive ratings—pass, warning, or fail—using an aggregate score of each dimension of evaluation.[1]

Common Sense evaluated Bark, Gaggle, GoGuardian, and Securly for their privacy practices; these evaluations were last updated in 2022 . Bark was given a warning and a score of 73 percent (Common Sense, 2022c), Gaggle was given a pass and an overall score of 91 percent (Common Sense, 2022b), GoGuardian was given a warning and a score of 57 percent (Common Sense, 2022b), and Securly was given a warning and a score of 63 percent (Common Sense, undated-d). It is important to emphasize that these are independent reviews using standards established entirely by Common Sense's research team.

---

[1] According to Common Sense, a *pass* means that a company "meets our minimum requirements for privacy and security practices," a *warning* means that the company "does not meet our recommendations for privacy and security," and a *fail* means that the company "does not have a privacy policy and should not be used" (Common Sense, undated-c).

CHAPTER 3

How Artificial-Intelligence–Based Tools Are Used for Student Suicide Risk Detection in Schools

In this chapter, we address our second research question: How are AI-based suicide risk monitoring programs being used in K–12 schools? We began by reviewing documents pertaining to the four major EdTech companies that sell AI-based student monitoring software to schools for suicide risk detection, including information available on their websites and information that each company has shared in response to congressional inquiries (Bark, 2023; Bason, 2021; Gaggle, undated-a; GoGuardian, undated; Madhusudan, 2021; Patterson, 2021; Securly, undated-b; Shinde, 2021). In this chapter, we summarize the information from those documents and from our semistructured interviews with representatives from a subset of these companies. The companies whose documents we reviewed were GoGuardian, Gaggle, Bark Technologies, and Securly; altogether, these companies service thousands of school districts and millions of students (Bark, 2023; Gaggle, undated-a; GoGuardian, undated; Securly, undated-b). We note that the EdTech marketplace is rapidly shifting, and other companies that have primarily produced online lessons and instructional content, such as Khan Academy, are also starting to offer suicide risk detection (Singer, 2023).

How Educational Technology Companies Describe Their Tools

Each of the four major companies describes its technology as an effective way to protect students, including by preventing suicide, self-harm, and harm to others. For instance, GoGuardian's Beacon is described as "a student safety solution built for K–12" that uses "data to drive meaningful interventions" (GoGuardian, undated). Similarly, Gaggle offers "Online Solutions for K–12 Student Safety" and reports that "Gaggle is Saving Lives" and that it will "stop tragedies with real time analysis and around-the-clock alerts" (Gaggle, undated-a; Gaggle, 2023). Securly offers products that "Identify at risk students and intervene early" to "protect your students against self-harm, suicide, bullying, and violence" (Securly, undated-b). Bark for Schools offers products that "monitor school issued accounts—for free" and allows schools to "get alerts when students might be in danger online" (Bark, 2023).

Several of the companies included in our review indicate that the goal of their tool is not to be a comprehensive solution to student suicide but to serve as a complementary component of that solution. For example, GoGuardian describes its Beacon program "as one data point of a school's overall suicide prevention program" (GoGuardian, undated; Shinde, 2021). GoGuardian adds that the company has developed its programs in consultation with suicide prevention organizations, such as the American Foundation for Suicide Prevention (GoGuardian, undated).

How Companies Flag At-Risk Students

Through our review of company documents and interviews, we identified that the EdTech companies have some commonalities in how they flag students at risk. The companies monitor student activity on school-issued devices and activity through school-administered accounts on personal devices. They also use proprietary machine learning algorithms, some of which include natural language processing, keyword analysis, and sentiment analysis to identify computer activity that suggests risk of self-harm (Securly, undated-a).

The monitoring conducted by these companies is *opt-out*, which means that the default setting is that the monitoring will be active on school-issued devices and accounts unless a caregiver or student proactively removes themselves from the program (Bason, 2021; Patterson, 2021; Shinde, 2021). Caregivers and students are typically notified that computer activity may be surveilled through the school's technology-use policy; this notice is provided when the school issues a device or account to a student. School districts or individual schools choose whether and how to notify and explain the use of AI-based suicide risk monitoring to caregivers and students. School technology-use policies typically do not include details about suicide risk monitoring programs, and there is evidence that many caregivers are unaware that these programs are in use (Laird et al., 2022).

EdTech companies take their own internal approaches to assessing the severity of suicide risk. When a risk is deemed sufficiently severe, an alert is passed to designated school contacts. The companies provide customization options for schools to determine the threshold of severity for when they will be contacted and which designated officials should be contacted. For instance, in response to congressional inquiry, the chief executive officer (CEO) of Securly stated, "We structure our flagging and alerting structures so that school administrators and officials are the focal point for alerting. Indeed, Securly's platform is both customizable and scalable by and for school officials . . . . Each school decides which of our products or services to use, how to configure them, and how broadly to deploy them as a supplement to existing school safety programs" (Madhusudan, 2021).

Although they do not share details of these algorithms, the companies do sometimes share aggregate numbers of alerts that are generated. For instance, in 2020, GoGuardian's CEO reported that Beacon generated approximately 10,000 alerts for active planning of suicide (Shinde, 2021). Gaggle's CEO reported that in the 2020–2021 school year, it issued more than 235,000 alerts regarding student activity that indicated risk of self-harm or violence (Patterson, 2021). We were unable to identify how much time school personnel spend responding to alerts.

These student activity monitoring programs operate continuously on school-issued devices and accounts, and alerts are generated and passed to school contacts and other designated contacts, such as law enforcement, on a continuous basis. However, the companies differ in their technical approaches to how they monitor school-issued devices and accounts. For instance, some programs monitor web browsing (e.g., GoGuardian [Shinde, 2021]), and others monitor email and chat functions (e.g., Gaggle [Gaggle, undated-c]). Securly Aware monitors student email, web searches, social media accounts, and other online activity (Securly, undated-a). Some of the companies have multiple internal human reviews before an alert gets passed to a school. The companies also offer tiers of service that offer different degrees of functionality and features. For example, GoGuardian offers three tiers: a starter plan that flags active suicide planning; a core plan that includes a broader variety of alerts and onboarding assistance; and a 24/7 plan that includes everything from prior plans and human review of all active planning alerts, along with other features (GoGuardian, undated).

The companies possess at least some personally identifiable information about students, such as name, email address, and device identifiers, along with the details and context of the computer activity that is determined to be risky (Bason, 2021; Patterson, 2021; Shinde, 2021). The companies have publicly stated that, although they use data they collect in a de-identified way to improve products and services, they do not sell or market student data to advertisers or other entities (Bason, 2021; Madhusudan, 2021; Patterson, 2021; Shinde, 2021). As discussed previously, the companies have also signed the Student Privacy Pledge 2020, which indicates that these companies are committed not to sell or market data. Nevertheless, there is an ongoing class action lawsuit in California brought by caregivers against Securly for allegedly illegally collecting and selling student data (Merod, 2023).

Importantly, the companies state that they neither collect demographic or other socioeconomic data, such as gender, race, or family details, directly from schools nor conduct research on the demographic impacts of their alerts. Thus, they cannot determine whether students of color or LGBTQ+ students, for example, are flagged for risky behavior more often than other students. For instance, Gaggle claims to "have no context or background on students when we first identify potential issues, ensuring that all students get the support they need—regardless of demographic factors like race, income level, or sexual orientation" (Patterson, 2021). Similarly, Securly does not collect "data on a student's race, ethnicity, or sexual orientation and therefore [does] not have access to information on how many flagged incidents come from students of color and/or LGBTQ+ students" (Madhusudan, 2021). Likewise, "GoGuardian cannot currently perform rigorous and precise analyses of algorithmic biases related to any student-level demographic or socio-economic data" (Shinde, 2021). However even if the companies do not proactively collect these data directly from schools, they might possess demographic data collected passively from students—for example, through race-, sex-, or disability-based search terms (e.g., "I think I'm gay") or when student computer activity is flagged and these demographics are revealed in the digital materials (e.g., photos).

After the companies issue the relevant alert to a school-designated contact, the school then determines how to proceed. However, in some cases, if a human review of the alert at the EdTech company has determined that there is an imminent risk to safety or if the alert is issued after school hours, the companies or the school district might directly contact law enforcement (Bason, 2021). According to research by the Center for Democracy and Technology, 37 percent of teachers whose school uses student activity monitoring software reported that when an alert comes in outside school hours, their school shares this information with law enforcement, which then responds to the alert (Laird et al., 2022).

The companies do not typically communicate with caregivers or students about safety alerts, although Bark, GoGuardian, and Securly have caregiver-facing apps that allow caregivers to monitor activity on school-issued devices (Bark, undated; GoGuardian, 2023; Securly Parents, undated). Typically, it is up to the schools to communicate information about student activity monitoring to the community. Several of the companies provide templates for schools to pass to caregivers and community along with recommendations for what should be done after an AI alert is issued. For example, Securly's response to an inquiry from Senators Elizabeth Warren, Edward J. Markey, and Richard Blumenthal states, "Securly provides a parent kit to all districts. The kits include details regarding the functioning and purpose of Securly's products and options for parental visibility through Securly's products" (Madhusudan, 2021). These EdTech companies also provide information on their websites for schools and caregivers about how the surveillance systems work, what data are collected, how the data are managed, and other resources related to mental health issues.[1]

---

[1] See for instance, Gaggle, undated-b.

CHAPTER 4

Benefits and Risks of Artificial-Intelligence–Based Suicide Risk Monitoring

In this chapter, we address our third research question: What is the perceived impact of these programs on students, what are the potential risks, and how can benefits be realized while mitigating risks? We begin by focusing on the potential benefits of AI-based suicide risk monitoring as described by interview respondents. We then turn to their potential risks and how to mitigate those risks, according to interviewees. This chapter includes quotations from our interview respondents and findings from previously published research. To protect their identities, we have assigned pseudonyms to each interview respondent. A table indicating the general role (e.g., school principal, health care provider) associated with each pseudonym is provided in Appendix C.

Potential Benefits

For the majority of school staff, health care providers, and EdTech company staff that we interviewed, the primary benefit of AI-based suicide risk monitoring is that it identifies students who might be experiencing mental health crises and who could be at imminent risk for suicide, particularly students who might not otherwise seek help. In addition, some school staff members and advocacy group staff and members whose children attend schools in which EdTech software is used told us that the software can also help caregivers to feel more comfortable about their children's online activities.[1] A 2022 Morning Consult poll found that almost 90 percent of caregivers, teachers, and administrators were very or somewhat supportive of the statement "how supportive, if at all, would you be if your school system were to consider using an online educational technology to help detect signs a student may be considering harming themselves" (Morning Consult, 2022).

Identifying At-Risk Students

The ability to identify students who might be at risk for self-harm was viewed as particularly important during what several of our respondents describe as a growing youth mental health crisis. The majority of school staff members in districts in which the software is used told us that the software provides an additional tool for identifying at-risk students.

For example, Jane, director of school safety for a large school district, told us that the "volume" of mental health challenges facing children—including students in her district—is unprecedented. As a result, she explained that using AI-based suicide risk monitoring in her school has been important because, if a student is experiencing a crisis, staff can "get that information early." Staff in Jane's district respond to suicide risk alerts from student activity monitoring software on a continuous basis, and their response can vary depending on the type of alert and the time of day it is received. Often, school staff respond to alerts by scheduling conversations with students to discuss the problems that they are facing and connect them to resources to provide help. If staff find that the student is indeed actively planning to harm themselves, they can call the school resource officer or law enforcement outside the school for additional assistance. In addition, alerts about potentially at-risk students received on evenings, weekends, and holidays when school staff are unavailable are forwarded to local law enforcement, which conducts welfare checks if necessary. She explained that if local law enforcement becomes involved, the law enforcement officers are "very well

---

[1] When discussing the interview data, we use *most* or *the majority* to refer to one-half or more of interview participants and *some* or *several* to refer to less than one-half of the respondents.

trained" to provide assistance to students who might be facing mental health challenges.

Eric, an EdTech company staff member who used to work in K–12 education, told us that as a school staff member "sometimes you can get really caught off guard if you don't have something in place" that monitors students' online activities. He said that "so many of the children are suffering silently" and AI software "helps in a way to help identify, get them supports, and hopefully get them into a setting where they can get the resources and help that they need."

Laura, a guidance counselor at a large high school that does not use AI-based suicide risk monitoring, felt that AI-based software could be helpful. She told us that many tips her office receives about students who might be facing mental health challenges come from other students or staff members who became concerned about someone's online activity, such as text messages or social media posts. Therefore, she "can see how that would be really helpful if a student said something, and it was flagged and able to be . . . funneled to the right person."

Tina, a doctor who works with children, told us that she has seen an increase in patients who have attempted suicide. She described three cases that she knew of in which AI programs flagged online searches conducted by children who were experiencing mental health crises and received emergency medical care as a result of the alert. In one case, a child was brought to the emergency department after an AI-based suicide risk monitoring program flagged their online searches on how to attempt suicide. The child was subsequently admitted to the hospital for mental health care, and the family was "grateful for this being recognized, and it was not on their radar at all." In another case, a child was also flagged for searches on how to attempt suicide and had overdosed on medication when the alert was sent. As a result of the alert, the child received emergency medical care. Tina emphasized that, again, because the child was not on anyone's "radar," the software was an effective tool for alerting others that they were experiencing a mental health crisis.

EdTech company staff members with whom we talked also emphasized that school districts can customize alerts to maximize the effectiveness of the tool. Adam, a technology specialist for one EdTech company, explained that its program can help categorize the level of crisis that a student might experience. For example, he explained that the program can help detect whether a student is "actively planning" a suicide and is searching for methods or is exhibiting more of a "curiosity" by searching for more general information about suicide. Schools can customize the level of alert they receive about a student's behavior (e.g., by excluding alerts that are likely to be curiosity-driven searches) and tailor their responses accordingly.

Respondents who thought that AI tools could be beneficial also emphasized that the programs should not replace face-to-face interactions with students. Instead, these programs were viewed as complementary tools to identify students in need. For example, Richard, a chief technology officer for a large suburban school district, emphasized that the software is not intended to replace in-person support but that "it is just one of the areas that we have in place to . . . just add another layer of how we can support students." Eric, the AI software company representative, emphasized that the program is designed to fill a "blind spot" for schools by adding to other in-person support resources that schools have at their disposal but not replacing those resources. Jack, a health care provider who researches youth and suicide risk, also emphasized the need for schools to "think about what they're going to do when they do receive an alert on a student." He emphasized that schools should have in-person counseling in place to assist students who might be experiencing mental health challenges.

Reassurance for Parents

Some respondents told us that, in addition to providing a tool for schools to identify at-risk students, the programs can provide reassurance to caregivers. Patricia, a member of an advocacy group focusing on technology use in schools, also has a child attending school in a district that uses AI-based suicide risk monitoring. She believes that the monitoring can provide "parents with visibility into what [their kid is] using their internet for and how much they're using their Chromebook." Thus, she said, the software "collaborates with the family and home life," and "if there are flags, [caregivers] can at least go check them out and address them at home."

Richard, the chief technology officer for a large school district, told us that his district was planning to add a feature to its AI monitoring that would allow caregivers to see how much time their children spend on school-issued computers and which websites they browse. He explained that "We want parents as partners, so a lot of times they need to have conversation with their student as much as [school staff] needs to have a conversation with their student." Thus, the programs were viewed by some respondents as having the potential to facilitate conversations that make caregivers feel more comfortable about their children's online activities.

Potential Risks and How to Mitigate Them

In addition to the potential benefits of these tools in helping schools detect student suicide risk, we also asked interviewees about potential trade-offs and advice for other schools or districts to consider before implementing these tools. Most of the advocacy group staff and members and some of the school staff who we interviewed discussed challenges associated with AI-based suicide risk monitoring software. The main themes from those interviews are discussed in this chapter. We also draw on previously published research to provide additional insight into our findings.

Student Privacy Violations

When we asked our respondents about potential challenges with AI-based suicide risk monitoring in schools, the most frequently expressed concern was the impact that the programs could have on student privacy. Adam, the technology specialist from an EdTech company, explained that companies work hard to protect student privacy. He told us, "Every school that uses—at least every public school that uses—our product, they have data privacy agreements that we have to agree to, and there's a whole host of security requirements and data retention [requirements]."

However, for other respondents, the programs posed a significant threat to student privacy. For example, Caroline, a staff member for an advocacy group that focuses on the use of technology in schools, explained that one of her biggest concerns about AI-based suicide risk monitoring is that it "creates a digital footprint for students." She went on to explain that this can be problematic because any behaviors flagged by the programs have the potential, if school districts were to choose, to become a part of a student's permanent school records. Caroline expressed concern that there is "not really an eraser button" for the data collected by the programs.

Limitation of Educational Opportunities

Respondents also noted that the data collected by schools could be used in ways that were harmful instead of helpful to students.[2] For example, Betsy, a school social worker, told us that her biggest concern about the use of AI software to monitor students is "how systems are tracking this data" and whether the data can also be used "against" students, such as through disciplinary actions. Although her school does not use any AI software, she became aware of a situation in a neighboring local school that raised concerns. She recalled that a student at the school was flagged by a software monitoring program because they conducted an internet search that contained the keywords "how to blow your head off." She told us that she felt the student's online activity was concerning and that the flag presented an opportunity for school staff to intervene if the student needed mental health support.

However, Betsy felt that instead of focusing on making sure the student was okay, school staff quickly moved to taking what she viewed as "punitive" measures. She said that school officials focused on whether the student was going to bring a gun to school to commit a crime. As a result, the student was removed from school grounds and was not allowed to return until they met a set of conditions, including seeking outside treatment services. In Betsy's opinion, the response by school officials—particularly the student's removal from school grounds—focused more on creating "consequences" for the student than providing mental health support.

Patricia, a respondent who is a member of an advocacy group and the parent of a child who attends a school in which the software is used, told us that she worries that the software could be used to make "assumptions" about students based on their online activities, such as their academic abilities. She also expressed concern that some students could be unfairly labeled

---

[2] It is important to note that, although EdTech companies provide software to schools, decisions about managing what activity is flagged by the software is often at the discretion of schools.

"underachievers" because of their monitored online activities. Her concerns stemmed from an experience with her own child. She said that when her child was in elementary school, an AI program flagged her child's online activity because one of their searches yielded results about the Ku Klux Klan. She said her child was just learning to use a computer and did not know what the Ku Klux Klan was or how the search results came up. Although she was able to intervene before her child faced disciplinary action, Patricia remained worried that the incident could be part of her child's school record.

A 2021 study by the Center for Democracy and Technology found similar concerns about the use of student activity monitoring software and student privacy (Center for Democracy and Technology, 2021). Its survey of teachers, caregivers, and students about the use of the software in schools found that 49 percent of caregivers and 40 percent of teachers surveyed were concerned that "Student online activity monitoring violates students' privacy." In addition, 57 percent of teachers and 61 percent of caregivers had concerns that activity flagged by the software could "bring long-term harm to students if it's used to discipline them or is shared and used out of context" (Center for Democracy and Technology, 2021).[3] However, the study found that 63 percent of the caregivers and 68 percent of the teachers they surveyed thought that "the benefits of student activity monitoring outweigh concerns about student privacy" (Laird et al., 2022).

For some respondents, concerns about student privacy were fueled by the lack of research on the impact of AI-based suicide risk monitoring in schools and a lack of regulation guiding how it is used to monitor student behavior. For example, Caroline, the staff member for the advocacy group who expressed concerns about the program creating a "digital footprint" for students, also told us that "it doesn't seem at this point like there's been any independent review of these technologies to see if the risks outweigh the potential benefits." She said she would like to see research on how programs "impact children's development and well-being."

---

[3] The survey respondents came from across the United States and consisted of 1,001 third- to fifth-grade teachers, 1,663 caregivers of students in K–12 schools, and 420 ninth- to 12th-grade students.

Concerns About Informed Consent

Some respondents also expressed concern about parental consent procedures. Through our discussions with school staff and EdTech company staff members, we learned that although companies distribute templates and guidance for gaining consent, the policies, decisions about what information to share with caregivers, and whether and how to obtain consent are the responsibilities of district officials. The school staff who work in districts in which the software is being used told us that their districts require a parent or guardian to consent to their student being monitored by the software when using a school-issued device. If caregivers opt out, the student cannot use a school-issued device but can participate in school activities using their own device, if they have one.

School staff who work in districts in which the software is used told us that, in general, they have faced very limited pushback, and a small number of families have opted out of participating. For example, Diana, a school administrator for a large public school district, told us that, although some caregivers expressed concern about the software when they initially learned that the district planned to use it on school-issued devices, just a few families opted out of participating after attending an information session. The software was required on school-issued devices, so she told us that the families who opted out were required to supply their own devices for use. Similarly, Richard, the chief technology officer for another school district, told us that, generally, his district gets "a lot of support" for the programs.

Theo is a member of an advocacy group that focuses on the use of technology in schools. He is also a lawyer and has done extensive research on the use of EdTech programs in schools. He told us that he feels that requiring families to consent to the use of AI software as a condition of using school-issued computers could be problematic. He explained that many students cannot fully participate in school activities if they do not have school-issued computers, and he said that he has consulted with families who were given few alternatives if they did not want their students to be monitored by this software. He told us that, in light of these experiences, he considers the consent process to be "manufactured." He also pointed out that this could be particularly problematic in public schools because "you have a right to public education," and attending a public school should not be "conditioned" on use of online activity monitoring programs.

Patricia, one of the advocacy group members with whom we talked whose son attends a school in which AI-based software is used, told us that she feels that students themselves should be able to decide whether they want to participate. She said, "ultimately, I think it is up to the child to participate or not" and that they should be specifically asked, "Do you want to be watched?"

Sarah, another advocacy group staff member, told us that she has found that many caregivers and students might not be fully aware of how the software works; some AI-based suicide risk monitoring tools operate in the background while students are using their computers and do not provide a "visual indication to the user" that the program is running. She told us, "It's like by design almost that you wouldn't know that it's on there." Parents and students might not understand the extent to which the software programs monitor their activities.

However, Tina, a health care provider who has experience working with children who have attempted suicide, pointed out that the way some AI-based suicide risk monitoring programs operate—in the background with limited indication that they're working—could be essential for identifying at-risk students. She explained, "Sometimes it does seem like the good aspect of this: the ability to identify children and adolescents who may not have disclosed these thoughts or plans to their families."

However, for some of our respondents, concerns about privacy and consent still overshadow the potential benefits of AI-based suicide risk monitoring. Caroline, one of the advocacy group staff members, called the situation a "double-edged sword," because, although the programs could help identify and intervene with at-risk students, families might have limited information about how much information the programs collect about students' lives. Similarly, Theo, the advocacy group member and lawyer, explained that because many EdTech software programs are designed to "continuously" observe students, they have the potential to collect large amounts of personal data. This continuous monitoring presents ongoing concerns about what this means for consent and privacy.

Disproportionate Impact on Students of Color and LGBTQ+ Students

Some respondents also worried that AI-based suicide risk monitoring might have a disproportionately negative impact on students who are members of underrepresented groups, particularly students of color and LGBTQ+ students. A staff member for an advocacy group focusing on the social impact of technology explained that the programs could potentially target already-vulnerable groups of students.

Although data on race are limited, some have expressed concerns that students of color could be disproportionately affected by surveillance-related disciplinary actions, particularly given that students of color already face disproportionately high rates of discipline in schools (Perera, 2022; Sabol et al., 2022). For example, Sarah, one of the staff members for an advocacy group, told us that, although some districts allow students the opportunity to opt out of participation in AI-based suicide risk monitoring by using their own devices, her organization's research has found that

> Black and Hispanic students, students who come from, you know, live in low, low-income areas . . . they are more likely to be dependent on a school-issued device and therefore not have like the means to essentially opt out of this tracking.

She told us that if the programs flag activity that leads to "disciplinary actions," members of those groups have "greater exposure than their peers who can essentially opt out." Additionally, she explained that because AI-based suicide risk monitoring alerts might lead to law enforcement involvement, they could play a role in "exacerbating" the "school-to-prison pipeline."

Although our research is exploratory, in the preceding section, two of our respondents provided examples of disciplinary interventions that were taken against students whose online activities were flagged by AI programs. In addition, Jane, the head of school safety, told us that law enforcement might be called in certain situations when a student is believed to be at risk—either when school staff need additional support or are unavailable to respond to alerts from AI-based software. These insights highlight areas in which the use of AI-based software could expose students to disciplinary action or law enforcement involvement.

In addition, concerns about disciplinary action also align with some evidence about student activity monitoring more generally. In a nationally representative survey of 860 ninth- to 12th-grade students, Laird et al. (2022) found that 55 percent of Latino students and 48 percent of Black students reported that they or someone they know at school "has gotten in trouble as a result of student activity monitoring," compared with 41 percent of White students.

Another particularly challenging issue is the potential for programs to track the online activities of LGBTQ+ students. A 2022 Vice News documentary on the use of AI-based suicide risk monitoring programs in schools featured several LGBTQ+ students who said that Gaggle had flagged their online activity around topics related to their identity (Vice News, 2022).[4] Because the online activity was flagged, the students were subject to disciplinary conversations with school staff and, in some cases, caregivers. These students were forced to disclose their sexual orientation to people to whom they might not have disclosed otherwise. The staff member for the advocacy organization who expressed concerns about AI programs contributing to the school-to-prison pipeline told us that her organization's research has also shown that program tracking could lead to outing LGBTQ+ students against their wishes, which in turn "inflicts harm on their mental health." It is important to note that the potential consequences for outing a student depend not only on that individual's situation (including their family and school community) but also on their state and local policies, which can prohibit teaching and discussing certain topics, such as sexual orientation, gender identity, and racial discrimination (Alexander et al., 2023; Polikoff et al., 2022; Woo et al., 2023). As this advocacy organization staff member pointed out, programs that are marketed as making students safer could have a negative impact on their overall well-being.

Sarah also told us she learned of a case in which a district flagged a student's search for information about the Defense of Marriage Act. She explained that the student "lived in a conservative school district that has their own values about gay marriage." The student was researching the topic

---

[4] The 2022 Vice News report focused primarily on Gaggle's EdTech software. The company responded in part by saying it was making changes to its algorithms.

because their parents were gay, and she felt that, by flagging the activity, the school used the software to "further impose their own values onto kids."

Caroline, an advocacy group staff member, echoed similar concerns regarding the impact of AI-based monitoring software on LGBTQ+ students. She told us that the programs could create a "potential for long-term harm for marginalized communities like the LGBTQ community." She used the example of LGBTQ+ students being outed by the programs potentially flagging searches related to their identity. She emphasized that children "deserve the right to identify how they identify on their own terms." These concerns align with findings from the 2021 study by the Center for Democracy and Technology on AI-based student online activity monitoring in schools. The study also found that 51 percent of caregivers and 47 percent of teachers were concerned about these programs outing LGBTQ+ students (Center for Democracy and Technology, 2021). In addition, Laird et al. (2022) found that LGBTQ+ students were more likely to report that they "got in trouble with the teacher or school for visiting a website or saying something inappropriate online." Their survey of 860 ninth- to 12th-grade students found that 56 percent of LGBTQ+ students reported having gotten in trouble for these online activities, compared with 44 percent of non-LGBTQ+ students.

It is important to note that the staff members from EdTech companies with whom we spoke rejected claims that the programs could play a role in perpetuating inequality by targeting certain groups of students. Eric, one of the EdTech company staff members, talked specifically about allegations that the programs target LGBTQ+ students. He told us that his company is "extremely sensitive to making sure that we are alerting on facts, and not disproportionately alerting on other factors." However, he pointed out the LGBTQ+ community is "at times more at risk statistically" for suicide, which could explain any patterns of apparent disproportionality. Staff members strongly emphasized that, because their companies do not collect demographic data, their algorithms are not driven by demographic characteristics. However, because companies do not collect demographic data, it is also difficult to measure disproportionality in program alerts.[5]

---

5 It is also important to note that we did not have access to any data or algorithms from EdTech companies.

False Positives, Problematic Responses, and Software Circumvention

Respondents also mentioned several other challenges. Some respondents expressed concern about the potential for programs to send false alerts and for responses to those alerts to be overly aggressive and to routinely involve law enforcement. A staff member for an advocacy group told us that, in her experience, "there's so many false positives with the surveillance technology." For example, Richard, a chief technology officer for a school district, told us that AI-based suicide risk monitoring can generate "a lot of false positives" when students are doing a school-based research project on suicide or other mental health challenges. Michael, a doctor who works on suicide prevention, told us that AI programs are "only as good as their inputs" and warned that program algorithms might rely too heavily on data from adults. Youth who are at risk for suicide could exhibit very different warning signs.

Jane, the director of school safety for a large school district in which the software is being used, acknowledged that there is "an element of human error in everything that we do." She emphasized the need for school personnel to look closely at the alerts they receive from AI-based suicide risk monitoring programs before acting. Richard, the chief technology officer for a large school district, explained that alerts from the program are an "indicator" but not an "absolute," and that staff are required to investigate alerts before deciding whether to take further action. Jack, the health care provider who researches youth and suicide risk, explained that using AI to detect suicide risk is a relatively new, developing area. Because of this, there are continued challenges associated with accuracy and false alerts. However, he also noted that he expects that models used to detect risk will "improve over time."

In addition to the concern about false positives, some respondents expressed concern about *how* schools choose to respond to alerts. Several school staff with whom we talked said that the programs might alert law enforcement if the activity is deemed particularly urgent or the alert is sent outside school hours when no school staff are available to respond. Sarah, a staff member for an advocacy group, pointed out that law enforcement involvement could potentially be problematic, particularly given concerns about whether the software perpetuates biases. She told us that schools "have routinized and systematized law enforcement presence." Although there is increasing concern about the physical presence of law enforcement in schools, she explained that AI-based monitoring can also further increase law enforcement presence, and law enforcement can become part of students' lives in a "very routine way through technology."

Finally, a few respondents discussed the potential for students to circumvent the software. For example, Richard told us, "our kids are smart" and "have learned that we're scanning their devices." They might try to use another device to avoid being monitored or alter the use of any language they think could be flagged. He also explained that students can use these strategies to mislead their caregivers about their online activities, making school intervention more challenging.

CHAPTER 5

Summary of Main Findings

In this chapter, we address our fourth and final research question: What are the best practices and recommendations for schools, caregivers, technology developers, and government seeking to use these technologies in K–12 schools while preventing potential harms? To do so, we integrate our findings across the report into several key findings. We then present a set of recommendations for schools, policymakers, and technology developers.

Main Findings

Artificial-Intelligence–Based Suicide Risk Monitoring Can Help Identify At-Risk Students and Provide Reassurance for School Staff and Parents

Our findings suggest that AI-based suicide risk monitoring could be useful as one component of a comprehensive school-based suicide prevention approach. Several respondents—particularly school staff and health care providers—provided examples of how alerts from AI-based suicide risk monitoring identified students who were at imminent risk for suicide and would not have been identified through other suicide prevention or mental health programs in the school. Given the extent of the mental health challenges among youth and limited resources available in schools and communities to address them, these alerts might provide new information that can allow proactive response and save lives. Additionally, we found that AI-based suicide risk monitoring can provide reassurance to caregivers that their students' online activities on school-issued devices are monitored.

Artificial-Intelligence–Based Suicide Risk Monitoring Could Have Benefits but Raises Questions About Privacy, Consent, and Equity

Our research shows that the use of AI-based suicide risk monitoring software comes with challenges and concerns regarding student privacy, consent, and equity. Many interview respondents worried about whether AI-based suicide risk monitoring programs used in schools compromise student privacy. These concerns were expressed by most of the parents and advocates and some of the school staff we interviewed but not by representatives of the AI companies. These programs are designed to collect sensitive information about students. Some respondents noted that information can become a part of a student's "digital footprint" at a young age. In addition, there is a lack of transparency about how school districts and schools use the student data collected by the programs.

Several respondents also expressed concern about the consent process for AI-based suicide risk monitoring, particularly because these programs are designed to operate passively without alerting students to their presence. Although EdTech companies provide guidance, school districts are responsible for crafting their own consent policies. In the districts in which school staff interviewees work, caregivers must consent to the use of surveillance software if their students use school-issued computing devices. If they do not consent, they are responsible for providing computing devices for their students to use, which could be problematic for several reasons. First, some of our respondents pointed out that caregivers might not fully understand the extent of the online activity monitoring when they consent. As discussed in previous chapters, details of the monitoring approach might not be provided and caregivers might only be notified in the context of a much broader and generic device-use policy. Second, most caregivers might not have a real choice to opt out of having their students monitored by the AI-based software because their students rely on school-issued computing devices to participate in academic activities. Third, students themselves are not always asked for consent, and many might not be fully aware of the extent to which their online activities are monitored or the purpose of that monitoring.

Some of our respondents also expressed concern that the use of AI-based suicide risk monitoring in schools could perpetuate existing inequalities. These programs might have a disproportionately negative impact on some students, particularly students of color and LGBTQ+ students. For example, students of color from lower-income backgrounds might be more likely to rely on school-issued computing devices. As a result, they might be less likely than White students to be able to opt out of online monitoring. Consequently, because data collected by programs can be used to take disciplinary action against students, this could fuel existing racial disparities in school disciplinary actions. Anecdotal evidence also suggests that some programs have algorithms that flag online activities by LGBTQ+ students, which could lead to some students being outed against their wishes or unfairly disciplined because of issues related to their identity (Vice News, 2022). It is important to note, however, that in the absence of data from schools and EdTech companies, we were unable to confirm whether or to what extent the AI-based tools are in fact leading to disparate outcomes for different groups of students.

There Is Limited Information, Research, and Regulation Surrounding the Use of Artificial-Intelligence–Based Suicide Risk Monitoring in Schools

We found that respondents' concerns about AI-based suicide risk monitoring were fueled by a lack of information, research, and regulations. As noted previously, schools might choose not to be transparent about what online activity is tracked, where it is tracked, when it is tracked, who sees the information, how data are stored, and how schools can be expected to respond to various types of online activity. Although a lack of transparency could help ensure that students are not circumventing the online monitoring, it also leads to numerous unanswered concerns on the part of caregivers, communities, students, and policymakers. Furthermore, there has been very little research on how AI-based suicide risk monitoring is used in schools, its effectiveness in accurately detecting youth suicide risk, and whether it perpetuates existing inequalities. This gap in the research leaves technology companies, school district leaders, caregivers, and legislators without the solid evidence needed to make decisions about how AI-based algorithms work, how alerts are handled, and other concerns. In addition, there are few laws and regulations at the federal, state, and local levels that govern the use of AI-based suicide risk monitoring tools in schools. Consequently, the way that these tools are implemented can vary widely depending on such factors as school district policies, the business model and policies of the EdTech company providing the service, and the resources available to the school and larger community.

EdTech company staff members and school staff in districts in which monitoring is used often emphasize that the programs are most effective when used in conjunction with other tools. School staff emphasized the importance of continuing to build relationships with students and providing in-person counseling services. Nearly all interview respondents noted that AI-based suicide risk monitoring should not be the only tool that schools use to navigate student mental health challenges, such as suicide risk. In addition, companies told us that they work hard to ensure that their programs' algorithms do not target marginalized groups of students, such as students of color and LGBTQ+ students.

However, a lack of systematic research on AI-based suicide risk monitoring makes it challenging to fully evaluate some of its potential risks. In addition, EdTech company staff members told us that they do not collect demographic data directly from schools, making it difficult to fully assess equity concerns. The lack of regulations also means that companies and school districts are largely left to regulate themselves—for example, by adhering to the aforementioned privacy pledge. To date, there are limited clear strategies for navigating the concerns raised by some of our respondents.

Recommendations

We recommend a robust plan for dissemination of information to facilitate decisionmaking across stakeholder groups. This section is organized around recommendations for schools, government representatives and policymakers, and EdTech companies. Our key findings and recommendations apply generally across EdTech companies rather than involving fine-grained distinctions about how each one operates.

Recommendations for School Districts

Engage Communities for Feedback

Conducting community engagement activities and integrating feedback on how these tools are used are essential for successful interventions in complex social systems, such as school districts, especially with respect to new technologies, such as AI. Per the Department of Education's report on integrating AI for educational purposes, "now is the time to show the respect and value we hold for educators by informing and involving them in every step of the process of designing, developing, testing, improving, adopting, and managing AI-enabled edtech" (U.S. Department of Education, 2023, p. 58).

Our research also shows that navigating alerts from AI software can be a complex process. Schools must decide which alerts to act on and who to inform when a student is potentially at risk for self-harm. We recommend a principle similar to the Department of Education's recommendation, which focuses on involving those responsible for mental health outcomes in schools. The Department of Education advises that school districts and schools engage a variety of stakeholders, including school personnel, pediatric and other community mental health providers, and local law enforcement, to inform them about plans for using the tools and seek their input on best practices for integrating these tools into the overarching set of interventions intended to support the mental health of students. These efforts should take place as part of the decisionmaking process, prior to the installation of AI-based student activity monitoring on school-issued devices. Indeed, communities should be engaged in the decision of whether this technology should be used in the first place. It is not a requirement or a foregone conclusion that schools use this technology, which, in the case of public schools, is purchased using taxpayer dollars. Furthermore, because the responses to the alerts and the messaging about the tools are the responsibility of the school, schools would also presumably bear responsibility for unintended harms resulting from a response to an alert (e.g., a violent police encounter, a botched response that results in a suicide). Ensuring that community members have had an opportunity to provide input on and be informed about how monitoring is used could help prevent adverse consequences for students and families and for school districts.

We have designed a process map (Figure 5.1) using our research that can be distributed to these community members so that they are aware of the

FIGURE 5.1

Process Map for Using Artificial Intelligence in Schools for Detecting Suicide Risk

K–12 schools around the country are using software that monitors students' computer activities to identify mental health and suicide risks. These are some key questions for schools, caregivers, and community members.

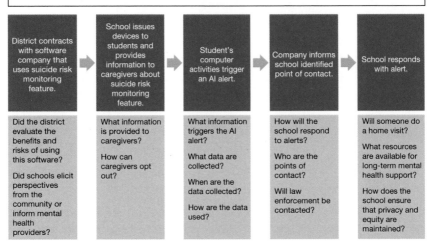

ways in which the school is using AI-based suicide risk monitoring. The process map also shows a set of key questions that these stakeholders might consider. This map is intended to inform the community and elicit feedback across each step about how the school is leveraging AI-based suicide risk monitoring.

Through these broader consultations, the use of AI-based monitoring in schools might not be seen purely as a technical solution to a complex problem, but a part of a complementary set of interventions in the broader educational system.

Clearly Notify Caregivers and Students About Suicide Risk Surveillance and Clarify Opt-Out Procedures

When engaging stakeholders, it is particularly important that caregivers and students understand what is being monitored, including activity on websites, email, and other messaging platforms, and how this monitoring might trigger alerts. Caregivers and students should also be provided with comprehensive information regarding how their data are being used, where the data are stored and for how long, who has access to the data, and whether the data can be shared with any third parties. Although this information might be provided in schools' device-use policy, it is worth flagging the specific role of AI-based suicide risk monitoring for caregivers to ensure that they understand the possible benefits and risks and are prepared to have conversations with students to help support their mental health. Whenever possible, caregivers should be provided with this information prior to the installation of AI-based suicide risk monitoring software on devices, making it a part of the decisionmaking process for opting out.

Establish an Effective and Consistent Process for Responding to Artificial-Intelligence Alerts

Schools develop their own processes to respond to AI-based suicide alerts. However, there are some best practices that all schools should consider. There should be a concerted and coordinated effort between school information technology and safety offices, other key school personnel (e.g., leadership, mental health support services), and community supports to respond to AI-based alerts. Recognizing that there might not be a one-size-fits-all approach, predetermined decision pathways of next steps should be established so that decisions are not being made ad hoc. Schools should ensure that a well-designed crisis response plan is in place to address any emergent situations relating to suicide risk. Schools should also limit reliance on law enforcement as part of the response (Beck, Reuland, and Pope, 2020). Efforts to ensure that crisis response mechanisms are in place continuously and that mental health resources are readily available are vital. If resources for responding to mental health crises are severely limited within a community, the school should consider, in concert with caregivers, whether to limit the use of AI-based suicide risk monitoring to be active only during school hours (i.e., alerts turn off on weekends and during school breaks). In the current environment, in which there is little research or policy to inform such decisions, this is a decision that will need to be made by each school or district based on how they weigh the relative risks and benefits of each option.

Our research builds on prior work showing that, along with its potential benefits for student mental health, AI-based monitoring software comes with threats to privacy, equity, and even safety (Laird et al., 2022). Before deploying such software, schools should establish safeguards to make sure that its use is restricted to cases in which a student can be helped, not harmed. Doing so will require comprehensive review of all aspects of implementation, from data security and storage to who is involved in responding to an alert and how. These processes might need to be tailored for each district and school based on their specific resources, student needs, and the policy context in which they operate (e.g., if state law requires schools to respond to information in a way that could compromise a child's safety or lead to punishment rather than support). All individuals involved in implementation should be trained to respond to alerts in a way that promotes positive, supportive intervention for at-risk youth rather than punishment or harm. In the absence of an established, validated training protocol, we recommend that school leaders connect with other school districts, mental health professionals, and EdTech companies and engage their own communities to develop or adapt training.

Track Student Outcomes from Suicide Risk Alerts

EdTech companies do not collect data on student outcomes or interventions that follow a suicide risk alert. However, schools should consider tracking this information, potentially in collaboration with researchers or evaluators, to examine the effectiveness of the alerts in improving mental health outcomes and preventing suicide and self-harm behavior. Schools can track the number of law enforcement interventions and disciplinary actions (at home and at school) that the alerts have triggered, the number of false positives and false negatives, and student outcomes from receiving assistance. EdTech companies should also examine whether certain groups of students are being flagged more often than others and why (e.g., because of their race, ethnicity, or identification as LGBTQ+). This information is critical to ensuring that implementation of these tools is ethical, effective, and equitable and that their potential harms are prevented. Schools need this information to refine their own workflows to ensure that their responses to suicide risk alerts are timely and effective.

Engage Students to Help Them Understand Mental Health Issues

In general, schools can use the integration of AI-based suicide risk alerts as an opportunity to initiate positive, healthy conversations with students about mental health issues and make them aware of school and community resources that are available to support them. Strategies could include building conversations into school assemblies, integrating conversations into parent-teacher events, making information available on district or school websites, and incorporating discussions into course curricula. These conversations can be part of developing a culture around mental health support rather than focusing on purely technical solutions. Schools should ensure that their messaging about and approach to these conversations is supportive and not punitive or stigmatizing. AI-based suicide risk alerts should be integrated into a larger, comprehensive suicide prevention approach that includes direct, face-to-face interactions between students and staff.

Review and Update Antidiscrimination Policies to Consider Use of Artificial-Intelligence–Based Technology

Schools should frequently revisit and update their antidiscrimination policies to reflect the use of EdTech, including AI-based suicide risk monitoring. These tools have the potential to disproportionately and negatively affect protected classes (e.g., race, gender, disability) (Laird et al., 2022); this was a fear that arose in several of our interviews and one that has been noted by policymakers (Office of Senator Elizabeth Warren, 2022). To protect their students from discrimination and respond to continually evolving technology and growing concern, schools must equip their civil rights coordinators, general counsel, and technology officers with the training and skills needed to understand the technology and its potential threats to civil rights. Once developed, these policies should be clearly communicated to school staff and caregivers.

Recommendations for Federal, State, and Local Government

Fund Evidence-Based Mental Health Supports in Schools and Communities

Government at different levels should provide additional funding to schools focused on evidence-based mental health support and suicide prevention for students, including the use of technology. Specific to suicide prevention, these efforts should include support for evidence-based programs across multiple levels of prevention (Singer, Erbacher, and Rosen, 2019). For example, early, universal approaches implemented even at the elementary-school level can help prevent suicide, and programs that focus on suicide risk mechanisms generally—which are usually also risk factors for other adverse outcomes, such as drug use and risky behaviors—can be resource-efficient approaches (Ayer et al., 2023; Wilcox et al., 2008). The federal government and many states have increased funding for these resources in response to growing need (U.S. Department of Health and Human Services, 2023), but data and our interviews suggest that additional support is needed (Bridge et al., 2023; Overhage et al., 2023).

The 2022 implementation of 988, the three-digit suicide prevention lifeline number, and high-profile examples of people experiencing a mental health crisis being killed by police (Bedayn and Slevin, 2023; Meko and Kriegstein, 2023; Treisman, 2020) have also prompted increased awareness of the importance of around-the-clock mobile crisis teams that can respond to emergent mental health crises rather than relying on law enforcement (Beck, Reuland, and Pope, 2020). However, many communities still lack access to such resources, meaning that it is the police who will most likely respond to AI-driven suicide risk alerts outside school hours. Providing funding for trained youth mobile crisis teams, however, could help schools that implement AI-based suicide risk monitoring programs mitigate potential risk for harm stemming from police interactions with youth in crisis.

Refine Federal Government Approaches and Standards for Privacy, Equity, and Oversight for Suicide Monitoring Systems

The current gaps in federal law give rise to serious privacy, equity, and oversight issues. The federal government could play a role in addressing these concerns through additional steps by both executive branch agencies and Congress.

At the executive level, the FTC has examined its authority to hold AI and other technology companies accountable for fairness and equity of their products and has encouraged companies to conduct discriminatory impact analysis and foster greater transparency through independent audits (Jillson, 2021). The privacy pledge signed by many of the EdTech companies that provide AI-based suicide risk monitoring software also references the FTC as the agency that could enforce the pledge (Future of Privacy Forum and the Software & Information Industry Association, undated-b). However, it is not clear whether and how the FTC has evaluated AI-based suicide risk monitoring in schools; given the privacy and equity risks to vulnerable student populations in need, this is an area that deserves further FTC attention.

Other executive branch actions could be supplemented to specifically deal with risks of the use of AI-based monitoring in schools. Efforts such as the White House *Blueprint for an AI Bill of Rights* do not clearly articulate how they apply to these student online activity monitoring programs (White House, 2022). The Department of Education report on the use of AI in schools does not discuss the use of student online activity monitoring software or the possible risks to privacy and civil liberties (U.S. Department of Education, 2023). Because of the widespread use of AI-based monitoring in K–12 schools and its potential risks, executive agencies should develop guidance and recommendations for how these tools are being integrated. Federal guidance is also lacking regarding the intersection of student surveillance software and existing civil rights protections in schools. Additional policies are needed to address how and whether civil rights protections apply.

Another option for addressing the key concerns would be for Congress to pass a federal comprehensive data privacy law and other legislation that would pertain to how companies monitor students' computer activity. Some congressional attention has focused on the specifics of AI-based suicide risk monitoring in schools, in particular in a report prepared by Senators Elizabeth Warren and Edward Markey (Office of Senator Elizabeth Warren, 2022)., There has been a lack of additional federal and other government engagement. Additional laws could consider privacy protections of student data beyond educational records, transparency, and independent audit requirements for EdTech companies to ensure that these tools have the intended impact of supporting students in need, as well as equity standards to ensure that there is not a disparate impact on marginalized communities.

Recommendations for Technology Developers

Continue Participation in School Engagement Activities

Per many of the recommendations described in the preceding sections, school feedback is essential for the most effective integration of these technologies. EdTech companies should continue and expand any existing engagement efforts, including supporting schools in their engagements with school boards, parent-teacher associations, and other fora in which they can notify communities about the use of the tools (including data privacy) and elicit feedback. These activities might also be opportunities to identify and disseminate other mental health resources for students in need of assistance.

In addition, as new AI capabilities such as affect or emotion recognition tools and AI mental health chatbots emerge and become more commercially available (Grant, 2023; Keierleber, 2022; Reardon, 2023), companies should proactively engage with diverse school leaders (e.g., from large and small districts; from rural and urban districts; those who have different roles, such as chief technology officer, superintendent, or principal) before integrating new tools to ensure that school communities understand and support their use.

Share Data to Allow for Evaluation of the Impact of Artificial-Intelligence–Based Monitoring Software on Student Outcomes

One of the strongest messages that came through our review of the literature and our interviews was that there is a lack of information about the extent to which the AI-based alerts avert suicide attempts and lead to improved student mental health, in addition to whether and how often they lead to negative or harmful outcomes. This information is critical for consumers (i.e., schools and caregivers) to be able to weigh the risks and benefits associated with these tools and for schools to understand how these programs should be implemented in the context of other mental health and suicide prevention activities. This information is also valuable for the companies themselves: Understanding the conditions under which their algorithms are accurate and helpful is necessary to improve the quality and utility of the products that they sell. Therefore, we recommend that these companies make their data available to independent researchers who can conduct rigorous and objective analysis—including linking these data to data from schools and health care systems—to fill this major gap in knowledge.

Develop Best Practices for Implementation of Artificial-Intelligence–Based Suicide Risk Monitoring

Another clear message stemming from our research findings is that best practices and industry standards need to be developed and publicized to assist EdTech companies in developing their approaches and to work with school districts and policymakers to implement these tools most effectively. However, more research is needed to develop and refine evidence-based guidelines. For example, best practices guidelines could cover the following areas:

- **narrow purpose of AI-based suicide risk monitoring:** One big concern is that AI-based suicide risk monitoring software might be used beyond identifying mental health issues, including for problematic activities, such as enforcing anti-abortion or anti-LGBTQ+ policies or tracking students' locations for discipline purposes (Merod, 2023). Companies should ensure that their products are only used for the narrow purpose of improving students' mental health without additional scope creep. Companies can commit to this narrow scope by integrating language into their contracts and terms of service to ensure that their products are not used for discipline, enforcing anti-abortion laws, or other potentially harmful purposes.

- **data protection and privacy:** EdTech companies collect sensitive information that might also be seen as valuable by cyberattackers, advertisers, and others. According to some research, more than 1,500 schools have been victims of cyberattacks (K12 Six, 2023), so it is important to ensure that these data are protected. There has also been litigation and questions surrounding what companies do with the data collected (Merod, 2023), although many EdTech companies have signed a privacy pledge (Future of Privacy Forum and the Software & Information Industry Association, undated-a). EdTech companies will need to maintain best practices around cybersecurity and data protection while being transparent and accurate about how they and others use their data.

- **accuracy of alerts:** Companies already take steps to improve the accuracy of their alerts to identify suicide risk. However, it is not possible for them to determine the true accuracy without further data collection on student outcomes and measurement of the alerts' external validity. Determining accuracy should be a high priority for EdTech companies. Companies should also conduct more research on the impact of their alerts to ensure that there is not a significant disparate impact or level of accuracy across demographic groups. They should also thoroughly examine how and when a human review of an alert is helpful or harmful, both in terms of accuracy and privacy risk.

- **improved responses to alerts:** Companies that have provided online activity monitoring to multiple, diverse districts across the country over many years have the benefit of learning from all of these applications of their software and offering guidance to school districts using those learnings. EdTech companies should consider how they can assist schools and the broader community in responding to alerts. This assistance might include working with mental health associations to develop guidelines for training school staff in how to respond to suicide risk alerts, such as which types of school staff should be responsible for different parts of the workflow and how to ensure that those responding to alerts are aware of how to prevent their response from resulting in harm (e.g., outing LGBTQ+ youth, punishment or disciplinary action, harmful police interactions). Assistance also might include making more resources available for school response.

- **transparency:** Companies can develop shared approaches and best practices for informing students, caregivers, and communities about their tools, such as additional details on how caregivers and students might opt in instead of requiring them to opt out.

Conclusions

We collected information on the trade-offs associated with school implementation of AI-based suicide risk monitoring software. Drawing from a review of the literature and other publicly available information (e.g., company responses to congressional inquiries) and semistructured interviews, we provided an initial look into these issues and developed a variety of recommendations for schools, policymakers, and technology companies. Further research is urgently needed to better quantify and define the risks, benefits, and impacts of this technology. In the meantime, this report provides an early foundation and guidance to enable schools and others to consider whether and how to use AI-based software to detect suicide risk among youth.

Methods

In this appendix, we detail the methods used for the literature review and semistructured interview data collection and analysis.

Literature Review

The literature review regarding the use of technology to prevent suicide in school-age youth was conducted by searching the following databases: Nexis, US News Stream, SCOPUS, Web of Science, Academic Search Complete, Business Sources Complete, ProQuest Military Database, Psychinfo, PolicyFile, PubMed, and Google Scholar. Search terms used consisted of suicid* and "risk detection" or screening; (AI or algorithmic) and (bias or equity or fairness or discrimination or racism); education technology; (AI or algorithmic) risk detection; GoGuardian; Gaggle; Securly; Bark Technologies or Bark for Schools; Lightspeed Systems; sentiment analysis; school surveillance or student surveillance; student monitoring; remote monitoring; child mental health; student safety; and student privacy. Inclusion criteria included any articles that discussed the use of technology to prevent suicide in school-age youth. We found 168 initial articles and screened out 36 articles for repetitiveness or nonrelevance. The remaining 132 articles were reviewed, summarized, and grouped into categories.

Qualitative Interviews

Recruitment

We used a multipronged convenience sampling approach to recruit study participants. Staff members from the four major EdTech companies that produce AI-based suicide risk monitoring software—Securly, Bark Technologies, GoGuardian, and Gaggle—were initially contacted via email. In two cases, we were provided with professional email addresses of key staff members through our team's professional networks. In the other two cases, we reached out to staff members identified through online searches. Ultimately, we completed interviews with staff members from three of the four major technology companies (75 percent response rate).

To recruit advocacy group staff and members, we began by identifying organizations that had either issued public statements or reports on the topic of school use of technology to monitor student suicide risk, or that are focused on youth and student suicide prevention. We began with four key organizations (two youth suicide–focused organizations, two technology use–focused organizations) and, through online searches and professional networks, were able to recruit three individuals for interviews (one from a youth suicide prevention organization, two from technology use–focused organizations, for a 75 percent response rate). These individuals then referred us to four individuals who represented other key stakeholder group perspectives, including parents and other respondents who had first-hand experience with the use of software in school districts, for a total of seven completed interviews from key stakeholder groups.

Initially, we planned to work with one school district that was implementing AI-based suicide risk monitoring for student suicide risk, and the study team submitted Institutional Review Board–approved study protocols and research questions to the district. However, after careful review, the district decided not to participate in the study out of concern that the topic might be too controversial. As a result, the study team decided to broaden the scope of the research to include viewpoints from a variety of school districts that serve different student populations.

We were interested in interviewing school staff from different roles (superintendents, principals, teachers, social workers, psychologists) who did and did not have experience using these tools in their schools and districts. These school staff were recruited in several ways. First, we collaborated with the National Center for School Mental Health, which conducts school-based mental health research, training, practice, and policy in districts across the country. The National Center for School Mental Health advertised the study on its social media (Twitter) and in its monthly newsletter. We received dozens of responses to the social media outreach but ultimately determined that only two responses were legitimately from school staff. The remainder were spam. No responses came from the newsletter. Simultaneously, we reviewed the websites of the four major technology companies and made a list of all of the school districts that were listed on their websites as implementing their tools ($N = 51$ districts). Through online searches, we identified the name and email address for the director of student support services in 44 of the districts. We then contacted the individuals in 11 of these districts, selected to obtain diversity in geography, urbanicity, and size. We received no responses from this outreach and determined that we should not invest further in this recruitment approach. The most successful approach for recruiting school staff was snowball sampling. At the end of each interview, participants were asked for recommendations for other individuals who might be interested in participating in the study. This approach yielded seven school staff interviews (see Appendix C for a full list of respondents).

In addition to these three major groups of interviewees, we interviewed three additional respondents who represented researchers, clinicians, and caregivers. These individuals were identified through professional networks and snowball sampling.

A total of 22 interviews were completed: EdTech company staff members ($n = 5$), advocacy group staff and members ($n = 6$), school staff ($n = 7$), and health care providers ($n = 4$).

Interview Data Collection

We conducted 22 semistructured key informant interviews. Interviews were approximately 60 minutes long, conducted remotely (via Zoom.gov), recorded, and transcribed. All interviews were guided by a semistructured interview protocol that covered a variety of topics, including the interviewee's job, position, or background; experience and familiarity with AI-based suicide risk monitoring; views of the monitoring tools (including benefits and risks, advantages and disadvantages); how these tools do or do not complement other school-based suicide prevention programs; best practices and lessons learned from using the tools; and recommendations for policymakers, schools, and technology companies.

At the end of the interview, participants were provided a 25-dollar gift card to thank them for their time. They were also asked for suggestions about who else to invite to participate in the study.

Interview Data Analysis

Interview transcripts were coded by members of our research team according to the themes relevant to our report. We developed a list of relevant codes using our research questions and interview notes. Coding families included the following:

- benefits of AI-based suicide risk monitoring software
- potential problems with AI-based suicide risk monitoring software
- company policies and practices
- best practices for using AI-based suicide risk monitoring software in schools
- best tools for dealing with student mental health challenges.

Once our list of codes was developed, a team of three coders was trained to systematically code interviews using Dedoose qualitative analysis software. As part of training, each coder separately coded the same interview. Doing so helped to establish inter-coder reliability and identify any challenges with the coding scheme. Once this process was completed, the list of codes was revised to clarify the meaning of some codes. Remaining interviews were coded by a single coder.

Once interviews were coded, we generated output of interview excerpts from Dedoose for the most frequently used codes. This output included codes on the benefits of using AI-based suicide risk monitoring software and the biggest challenges associated with the software, such as privacy and consent concerns. The output was then used to identify main themes and write up findings for this report.

Interview Protocols

This appendix contains the interview protocols that we used for the study.

EdTech Company Staff and Leader Protocol

1. What is your current job position?
2. How long have you been working in your current position?
3. Tell us about your company's AI suicide prevention tools.
   a. What are the goals of the tools?
   a. Who are the intended users?
   a. How many schools or districts are using these tools?
4. How does the tool/program identify a possible case of self-harm/suicide risk? (**Probe:** What data sources/indicators are used?)
5. How accurate is the tool at identifying cases? (**Probe:** What tools do you use to assess accuracy, if any?)
6. What are the biggest strengths of the tool?
7. Does the tool have any weaknesses? (**Probe:** If yes, what are the weaknesses?)
8. How do you assess for potential bias in the identification of potential self-harm/suicide risk cases? By bias we mean things like differences in identification of cases by race, gender identity or other background characteristics.
9. What guidance do you give to schools about using the tool?
   a. What guidance do you give schools for how they should respond to alerts?
10. What guidance do you give to parents and students about the tool?
    a. What is the process for parents/students to opt-in or -out of using the tool?

11. Do you engage with the local community about the tool? (**Probe:** If yes, what type of engagement?)
12. Overall, how effective is the tool in preventing self-harm? (**Probe:** What data sources/indicators do you use to assess effectiveness?)
13. Can you share any feedback (positive, negative or neutral) on the tools that you've received from schools, families, policymakers, or other stakeholders?

We have reached the end of the interview. Are there any issues that you wanted to discuss that we did not ask about? (**If yes:** Please explain.)

To thank you for your time we would like to send you a $25 Amazon gift card code. We have your email address as [fill in if available]. Is this the best place to send the code?

Alternative email [or mailing address if physical gift card is preferred]:

Can you recommend anyone else for us to talk with? [specify: parents, school staff, etc.]

Thank you so much for your time today.

Advocacy Group Staff and Member Protocol

1. What is your current job position?
2. How long have you been affiliated with [name of organization]?
3. Why did you decide to become involved with [name of organization]?
4. What are the organization's goals?
   a. **Probe:** What is your organization's position on AI surveillance software, such as GoGuardian and Gaggle, in schools?
   b. **Probe:** What about AI surveillance software for the purposes of identifying students who may be at risk for suicide?
5. Who are your organization's members/constituents?
6. In your opinion, are there advantages to using AI surveillance software in schools? (If yes: probe)
   a. **Probe:** What are specific advantages of using it for suicide risk detection and prevention?
7. What are the disadvantages and risks of using AI surveillance software in schools?

    a.   **Probe:** What are specific disadvantages of using it for suicide risk detection and prevention?

8.   What do you consider to be best practices for using these tools for suicide risk detection and prevention?

    a.   **Probe:** Are there any software companies that are following some or all of these best practices? (If yes: can you tell us about the company and what they're doing?)

9.   Has your organization talked with AI surveillance software companies about the impact of their programs?

    a.   **Probe:** Can you tell us about the issues that were discussed?

10.   Based on your organization's experiences, what do you think members of the following groups should know about the use of AI surveillance software in schools?

    a.   Parents
    b.   Students
    c.   Teachers
    d.   School administrators
    e.   Mental health providers
    f.   Police
    g.   Emergency department providers
    h.   Pediatricians
    i.   Policymakers (local, state, federal)

11.   Should local or state governments take steps to regulate the use of AI surveillance software companies?

    a.   **If yes:** What steps should they take?
    b.   **If no:** Why don't you think they should take any steps regulate the use of software?

12.   Other than using AI surveillance software, what strategies can schools use to support students facing mental health challenges?

We have reached the end of the interview. Are there any issues that you wanted to discuss that we did not ask about? (**If yes:** Please explain.)

To thank you for your time we would like to send you a $25 Amazon gift card code. We have your email address as [fill in if available]. Is this the best place to send the code?

Alternative email [or mailing address if physical gift card is preferred]:

Can you recommend anyone else for us to talk with? [specify: parents, school staff, etc.]

Thank you so much for your time today.

School Staff and Leader Interview Protocol

1. What is your current job?
2. How long have you been working for [name of school/district]?
3. What are some of the things you like most about your job?
4. What are some of the biggest challenges you face in your job?
5. What types of support services does [name of school/district] provide for students experiencing problems at school? This includes academic challenges and mental and physical health challenges.
   a. Are there specific programs at your school? (**Probe:** Do you know of any suicide prevention programs at your school?)
   b. Is there enough support available? (**Probe:** Please explain.)
   c. Are there improvements that could be made to support services? (**Probe:** Please explain.)
6. Do students in your school use school issued computer devices?
   a. If yes, what do they use it for?
   b. If no, what do they use instead?
   c. What are the biggest challenges to students using school issued computer devices?
7. [GoGuardian Beacon/Gaggle] is a program that can be loaded on a school-issued computer that monitors students' online activity to identify a risk of self-harm, suicide, or harm to others. Are you familiar with this program?
   a. If yes, how did you learn about it?
   b. If yes, do you use [GoGuardian Beacon/Gaggle] in your [district/school/classroom]? If so, how?
8. Have you received information about [GoGuardian Beacon/Gaggle] from your [district/school]?

If yes:

What type of information did you receive? (**Probe:** Was the information conveyed in a way that was easy to understand? Was there any information you wanted but did not receive?)

How do you think the program fits within the school's overall suicide prevention strategy or with other suicide prevention efforts going on at the school (if applicable)?

9. What do you think are some of the benefits of the program? (**Probe:** Does it help students do their work? Can it help identify students with mental health challenges?)

10. What are some potential problems with the program?

11. Have you discussed the program with your students? (**Probe:** If yes, what issues did you discuss?)

12. Have you discussed the program with parents/guardians of your students? (**Probe:** If yes, what issues did you discuss?)

13. Have you talked with other school staff members or administrators about the program? (**Probe:** If yes, what issues did you discuss?)

14. Have you ever been involved in contacting a parent or guardian about a possible problem their child was facing that was detected by [GoGuardian Beacon/Gaggle]?

    a. **If yes:** Can you tell us about what happened?

    b. How satisfied were you with the school's response?

    c. Was there anything that could have been improved about how the software was used?

15. What other steps could your school or district take to improve mental health outcomes for students?

We have reached the end of the interview. Are there any issues that you wanted to discuss that we did not ask about? (**If yes:** Please explain.)

To thank you for your time we would like to send you a $25 Amazon gift card code. We have your email address as [fill in if available]. Is this the best place to send the code?

Alternative email [or mailing address if physical gift card is preferred]:

Can you recommend anyone else for us to talk with? [specify: parents, school staff, etc.]

Thank you so much for your time today.

Study Respondents

In this appendix, we provide a list of respondents who were interviewed as part of our study (Table C.1).

TABLE C.1
List of Respondents

Pseudonym[a]	Description[b]
School staff members	
Betsy	School social worker, large public school district
Charles	Administrator, large public school district
Diana	Administrator, large urban school district
Jane	Director of school safety, large public school district
Laura	Guidance counselor, large public high school
Richard	Chief technology officer, large public school district
William	Chief technology officer, large public school district
Health care providers	
Jack	Doctor and researcher
Michael	Doctor, suicide prevention
Nicole	Social worker
Tina	Doctor, pediatrics
EdTech company staff	
Adam	Technology specialist, EdTech company
Douglas	Chief executive officer, EdTech company
Eric	Representative, EdTech company

Table C. 1—Continued

Pseudonym[a]	Description[b]
Maria	Representative, EdTech company
Zachary	Chief executive officer, EdTech company
Advocacy group staff and members	
Caroline	Staff member, advocacy group on technology in schools
Isabel	Member, advocacy group focused on the use of technology in schools; parent
Mary	Member, advocacy group on technology in schools; lawyer
Patricia	Member, advocacy group focused on the use of technology in schools; parent
Sarah	Staff member, advocacy group on technology in schools
Theo	Member, advocacy group focused on technology use and children

[a] All respondents were assigned pseudonyms to protect their identities.

[b] Some job descriptions have been generalized to protect respondents' identities.

Abbreviations

AI	artificial intelligence
CEO	chief executive officer
COVID-19	coronavirus disease 2019
EdTech	educational technology
FTC	Federal Trade Commission
K–12	kindergarten through 12th grade
LGBTQ+	lesbian, gay, bisexual, transgender, queer, or questioning

References

Agency for Healthcare Research and Quality, *2022 National Healthcare Quality and Disparities Report*, 2022.

Alexander, Taifha, LaToya Baldwin Clark, Kyle Reinhard, and Noah Zatz, *CRT Forward: Tracking the Attack on Critical Race Theory*, UCLA School of Law, 2023.

Austin, Ashley, Shelley L. Craig, Sandra D'Souza, and Lauren B. McInroy, "Suicidality Among Transgender Youth: Elucidating the Role of Interpersonal Risk Factors," *Journal of Interpersonal Violence*, Vol. 37, Nos. 5–6, March 2022.

Ayer, Lynsay, and Lisa J. Colpe, "The Key Role of Schools in Youth Suicide Prevention," *Journal of the American Academy of Child and Adolescent Psychiatry*, Vol. 62, No. 1, January 2023.

Ayer, Lynsay, Clare Stevens, Eve Reider, Belinda Sims, Lisa Colpe, and Jane Pearson, "Preventing Youth Suicide: Potential 'Crossover Effects' of Existing School-Based Programs," *Prevention Science*, Vol. 24, No. 2, February 2023.

Bark, homepage, undated. As of October 12, 2023:
https://www.bark.us

Bark, "Internet Safety for Students and Schools—Bark for Schools," webpage, 2023. As of October 12, 2023:
https://www.bark.us/schools

Barry, Ellen, "Can Smartphones Help Predict Suicide?" *New York Times*, September 30, 2022.

Barua, Prabal Datta, Jahmunah Vicnesh, Oh Shu Lih, Elizabeth Emma Palmer, Toshitaka Yamakawa, Makiko Kobayashi, and Udyavara Rajendra Acharya, "Artificial Intelligence Assisted Tools for the Detection of Anxiety and Depression Leading to Suicidal Ideation in Adolescents: A Review," *Cognitive Neurodynamics*, 2022.

Bason, Brian, Bark for Schools response to inquiry, letter to Elizabeth Warren, Edward J. Markey and Richard Blumenthal, October 22, 2021.

Beck, Jackson, Melissa Reuland, and Leah Pope, *Behavioral Health Crisis Alternatives: Shifting from Police to Community Responses*, Vera Institute of Justice, 2020.

Bedayn, Jess, and Colleen Slevin, "Family of Colorado Man Killed by Police During Mental Health Crisis Gets $19 Million Settlement," *PBS News Hour*, May 23, 2023.

Bernert, Rebecca A., Amanda M. Hilberg, Ruth Melia, Jane Paik Kim, Nigam H. Shah, and Freddy Abnousi, "Artificial Intelligence and Suicide Prevention: A Systematic Review of Machine Learning Investigations," *International Journal of Environmental Research and Public Health*, Vol. 17, No. 16, 2020.

Bharti, Shubham, Arun Kumar Yadav, Mohit Kumar, and Divakar Yadav, "Cyberbullying Detection from Tweets Using Deep Learning," *Kybernetes*, Vol. 51, No. 9, 2022.

Bilsen, Johan, "Suicide and Youth: Risk Factors," *Frontiers in Psychiatry*, Vol. 9, 2018.

Blodgett, Su Lin, and Brendan O'Connor, "Racial Disparity in Natural Language Processing: A Case Study of Social Media African-American English," *arXiv*, 2017.

Bridge, Jeffrey A., Donna A. Ruch, Arielle H. Sheftall, Hyeouk Chris Hahm, Victoria M. O'Keefe, Cynthia A. Fontanella, Guy Brock, John V. Campo, and Lisa M. Horowitz, "Youth Suicide During the First Year of the COVID-19 Pandemic," *Pediatrics*, Vol. 151, No. 3, March 2023.

Byars, Jason, Emily Graybill, Quynh Wellons, and Lonny Harper, "Monitoring Social Media and Technology Use to Prevent Youth Suicide and School Violence," *Contemporary School Psychology*, Vol. 24, No. 3, 2020.

Center for Democracy and Technology, *Student Activity Monitoring Software: Research Insights and Recommendations*, 2021.

Centers for Disease Control and Prevention, "Injury Counts and Rates," dataset, 2021. As of October 12, 2023: https://wisqars.cdc.gov/reports/

Centers for Disease Control and Prevention, *Youth Risk Behavior Survey: Data Summary and Trends Report*, 2022.

Chung, Anna Woorim, "How Automated Tools Discriminate Against Black Language," *Civic Media*, January 24, 2019.

Coley, R. Yates, Eric Johnson, Gregory E. Simon, Maricela Cruz, and Susan M. Shortreed, "Racial/Ethnic Disparities in the Performance of Prediction Models for Death by Suicide After Mental Health Visits," *JAMA Psychiatry*, Vol. 78, No. 7, July 2021.

Common Sense, homepage, undated-a. As of October 12, 2023: https://privacy.commonsense.org

Common Sense, "Evaluation Process," webpage, undated-b. As of October 12, 2023: https://privacy.commonsense.org/resource/evaluation-process

Common Sense, "Rating Questions," webpage, undated-c. As of October 12, 2023:
https://privacy.commonsense.org/resource/rating-questions

Common Sense, "Securly," webpage, undated-d. As of October 12, 2023:
https://www.commonsense.org/education/reviews/securly

Common Sense, "Privacy Evaluation for Bark," webpage, last updated April 1, 2022a. As of October 12, 2023:
https://privacy.commonsense.org/evaluation/Bark

Common Sense, "Privacy Evaluation for GoGuardian (Product)," webpage, last updated August 30, 2022b. As of October 12, 2023:
https://privacy.commonsense.org/evaluation/GoGuardian-Product

Common Sense, "Privacy Evaluation for Gaggle," webpage, last updated September 6, 2022c. As of October 12, 2023:
https://privacy.commonsense.org/evaluation/gaggle

Cwik, Mary F., Victoria M. O'Keefe, and Emily E. Haroz, "Suicide in the Pediatric Population: Screening, Risk Assessment and Treatment," *International Review of Psychiatry*, Vol. 32, No. 3, May 2020.

De Choudhury, Munmun, Michael Gamon, Scott Counts, and Eric Horvitz, "Predicting Depression via Social Media," *Proceedings of the Seventh International AAAI Conference on Web and Social Media*, Vol. 7, No. 1, August 3, 2021.

D'Hotman, Daniel, and Erwin Loh, "AI Enabled Suicide Prediction Tools: A Qualitative Narrative Review," *BMJ Health and Care Informatics*, Vol. 27, No. 3, October 2020.

Doan, Sy, Elizabeth D. Steiner, Rakesh Pandey, and Ashley Woo, *Teacher Well-Being and Intentions to Leave: Findings from the 2023 State of the American Teacher Survey*, RAND Corporation, RR-A1108-8, 2023. As of October 12, 2023:
https://www.rand.org/pubs/research_reports/RRA1108-8.html

Federal Communications Commission, "Children's Internet Protection Act (CIPA)," webpage, last updated December 30, 2019. As of October 12, 2023:
https://www.fcc.gov/consumers/guides/childrens-internet-protection-act

Ferrer, Xavier, Tom van Nuenen, Jose M Such, Mark Coté, and Natalia Criado, "Bias and Discrimination in AI: A Cross-Disciplinary Perspective," *IEEE Technology and Society Magazine*, Vol. 40, No. 2, June 2021.

Future of Privacy Forum and the Software & Information Industry Association, "K-12 School Service Provider Pledge to Safeguard Student Privacy 2020," webpage, undated-a. As of October 12, 2023:
https://studentprivacypledge.org/privacy-pledge-2-0/

Future of Privacy Forum and the Software & Information Industry Association, "Pledge 2020 Guidelines," webpage, undated-b. As of October 12, 2023:
https://studentprivacypledge.org/faqs/

Gaggle, homepage, undated-a. As of October 12, 2023:
www.gaggle.net

Gaggle, "Gaggle Content," webpage, undated-b. As of October 12, 2023:
https://www.gaggle.net/content

Gaggle, "Gaggle Safety Management," webpage, undated-c. As of October 12, 2023:
https://www.gaggle.net/safety-management

Gaggle, *Guardian Angel or Big Brother? What Educators Really Think of Student Safety Platforms*, 2023.

Gellman, Barton, and Sam Adler-Bell, "The Disparate Impact of Surveillance," The Century Foundation, December 21, 2017.

GoGuardian, "GoGuardian Beacon," webpage, undated. As of October 12, 2023:
https://www.goguardian.com/beacon

GoGuardian, "Guardians: What Student Data Can I See Using GoGuardian Parent?" webpage, May 17, 2023.

Grant, Nico, "Google Tests an A.I. Assistant That Offers Life Advice," *New York Times*, August 16, 2023.

Hankerson, DeVan L., Cody Venzke, Elizabeth Laird, Hugh Grant-Chapman, and Dhanaraj Thakur, *Online and Observed: Student Privacy Implications of School-Issued Devices and Student Activity Monitoring Software*, Center for Democracy and Technology, 2021.

Haroz, Emily E., Colin G. Walsh, Novalene Goklish, Mary F. Cwik, Victoria O'Keefe, and Allison Barlow, "Reaching Those at Highest Risk for Suicide: Development of a Model Using Machine Learning Methods for Use with Native American Communities," *Suicide and Life-Threatening Behavior*, Vol. 50, No. 2, April 2020.

Hitczenko, Kasia, Henry R. Cowan, Matthew Goldrick, and Vijay A. Mittal, "Racial and Ethnic Biases in Computational Approaches to Psychopathology," *Schizophrenia Bulletin*, Vol. 48, No. 2, March 2022.

Hoffmann, Jennifer A., Megan M. Attridge, Michael S. Carroll, Norma-Jean E. Simon, Andrew F. Beck, and Elizabeth R. Alpern, "Association of Youth Suicides and County-Level Mental Health Professional Shortage Areas in the US," *JAMA Pediatrics*, Vol. 177, No. 1, January 2023.

Jillson, Elisa, "Aiming for Truth, Fairness, and Equity in Your Company's Use of AI," *Federal Trade Commission Business Blog*, April 19, 2021.

K12 Six, "The K–12 Cyber Incident Map," webpage, last updated February 13, 2023. As of October 12, 2023:
https://www.k12six.org/map

Kapur, Supriya, "Reducing Racial Bias in AI Models for Clinical Use Requires a Top-Down Intervention," *Nature Machine Intelligence*, Vol. 3, No. 6, June 2021.

Keierleber, Mark, "Young and Depressed? Try Woebot! The Rise of Mental Health Chatbots in the US," *The Guardian*, April 13, 2022.

Kelly, Yvonne, Afshin Zilanawala, Cara Booker, and Amanda Sacker, "Social Media Use and Adolescent Mental Health: Findings from the UK Millennium Cohort Study," *EClinicalMedicine*, Vol. 6, 2018.

King, Cheryl A., David Brent, Jacqueline Grupp-Phelan, T. Charles Casper, J. Michael Dean, Lauren S. Chernick, Joel A. Fein, E. Melinda Mahabee-Gittens, Shilpa J. Patel, Rakesh D. Mistry, Susan Duffy, Marlene Melzer-Lange, Alexander Rogers, Daniel M. Cohen, Allison Keller, Rohit Shenoi, Robert W. Hickey, Margaret Rea, Mary Cwik, Kent Page, Taylor C. McGuire, Jiebiao Wang, Robert Gibbons, and Pediatric Emergency Care Applied Research Network, "Prospective Development and Validation of the Computerized Adaptive Screen for Suicidal Youth," *JAMA Psychiatry*, Vol. 78, No. 5, 2021.

Laird, Elizabeth, Hugh Grant-Chapman, Cody Venzke, and Hannah Quay-de la Vallee, *Hidden Harms: The Misleading Promise of Monitoring Students Online*, Center for Democracy and Technology, 2022.

Lejeune, Alban, Aziliz Le Glaz, Pierre-Antoine Perron, Johan Sebti, Enrique Baca-Garcia, Michel Walter, Christophe Lemey, and Sofian Berrouiguet, "Artificial Intelligence and Suicide Prevention: A Systematic Review," *European Psychiatry*, Vol. 65, No. 1, February 2022.

Madhusudan, Bharath, Securly response to inquiry, letter to Elizabeth Warren, Edward J. Markey, and Richard Blumenthal, October 15, 2021.

McCarthy, John F., Samantha A. Cooper, Kallisse R. Dent, Aaron E. Eagan, Bridget B. Matarazzo, Claire M. Hannemann, Mark A. Reger, Sara J. Landes, Jodie A. Trafton, Michael Schoenbaum, and Ira R. Katz, "Evaluation of the Recovery Engagement and Coordination for Health—Veterans Enhanced Treatment Suicide Risk Modeling Clinical Program in the Veterans Health Administration," *JAMA Network Open*, Vol. 4, No. 10, 2021.

Mehrabi, Ninareh, Fred Morstatter, Nripsuta Saxena, Kristina Lerman, and Aram Galstyan, "A Survey on Bias and Fairness in Machine Learning," *ACM Computing Surveys*, Vol. 54, No. 6, July 2021.

Meko, Hurubie, and Brittany Kriegstein, "He Was Mentally Ill and Armed. The Police Shot Him Within 28 Seconds," *New York Times*, March 30, 2023.

Merod, Anna, "Class Action Lawsuit Claims School Security Software Company Violated Students' Privacy," *K–12 Dive*, July 21, 2023.

Morning Consult, *EdTech in Schools: Creating Safer Digital Learning Environments*, 2022.

Nguyen, Tuan D., Chanh B. Lam, and Paul Bruno, *Is There a National Teacher Shortage? A Systematic Examination of Reports of Teacher Shortages in the United States*, Annenberg Institute at Brown University, 2022.

Office of Senator Elizabeth Warren, "Warren, Markey Investigation Finds That EdTech Student Surveillance Platforms Need Urgent Federal Action to Protect Students," press release, March 30, 2022.

Overhage, Lindsay, Ruth Hailu, Alisa B. Busch, Ateev Mehrotra, Kenneth A. Michelson, and Haiden A. Huskamp, "Trends in Acute Care Use for Mental Health Conditions Among Youth During the COVID-19 Pandemic," *JAMA Psychiatry*, Vol. 80, No. 9, 2023.

Patterson, Jeff, Gaggle response to inquiry, letter to Elizabeth Warren, Edward J. Markey, and Richard Blumenthal, October 12, 2021.

Perera, Rachel M., "Reforming School Discipline: What Works to Reduce Racial Inequalities?" Brookings Institution, 2022.

Polikoff, Morgan, Daniel Silver, Amie Rapaport, Anna Saavedra, and Marshall Garland, *A House Divided? What Americans Really Think About Controversial Topics in Schools*, University of Southern California, 2022.

Reardon, Sara, "AI Chatbots Could Help Provide Therapy, but Caution Is Needed," *Scientific American*, June 14, 2023.

Ridout, Kathryn K., Mubarika Alavi, Samuel J. Ridout, Maria T. Koshy, Sameer Awsare, Brooke Harris, David R. Vinson, Constance M. Weisner, Stacy Sterling, and Esti Iturralde, "Emergency Department Encounters Among Youth With Suicidal Thoughts or Behaviors During the COVID-19 Pandemic," *JAMA Psychiatry*, Vol. 78, No. 12, 2021.

Sabol, Terri J., Courtenay L. Kessler, Leoandra Onnie Rogers, Amelie Petitclerc, Jamilah Silver, Margaret Briggs-Gowan, and Lauren S. Wakschlag, "A Window into Racial and Socioeconomic Status Disparities in Preschool Disciplinary Action Using Developmental Methodology," *Annals of the New York Academy of Sciences*, Vol. 1508, No. 1, February 2022.

Samji, Hasina, Judy Wu, Amilya Ladak, Caralyn Vossen, Evelyn Stewart, Naomi Dove, David Long, and Gaelen Snell, "Mental Health Impacts of the COVID-19 Pandemic on Children and Youth—A Systematic Review," *Child and Adolescent Mental Health*, Vol. 27, No. 2, 2022.

Securly, "Aware: Understand Your Students' Mental Health, and Help Those Who Need It Most," product brief, undated-a. As of October 12, 2023: https://www.securly.com/site/assets/product-briefs/aware.pdf

Securly, "Support Student Mental Health and Wellness with Securly," webpage, undated-b. As of October 12, 2023: https://www.securly.com/solutions/student-wellness

Securly Parents, homepage, undated. As of October 12, 2023: https://www.securly.com/home-parent

Shaw, Jennifer L., Julie A. Beans, Carolyn Noonan, Julia J. Smith, Mike Mosley, Kate M. Lillie, Jaedon P. Avey, Rebecca Ziebell, and Gregory Simon, "Validating a Predictive Algorithm for Suicide Risk with Alaska Native Populations," *Suicide and Life-Threatening Behavior*, Vol. 52, No. 4, August 2022.

Shinde, Advait, GoGuardian response to inquiry, letter to Elizabeth Warren, Edward J. Markey, and Richard Blumenthal, October 26, 2021.

Shree, Shalini, and Arshdeep Singh Chudhey, "A Peek into One's Emotion Through Pen: Analyzing Individual's Emotion Through Their Thoughts Expressed on Various Social Media Platforms Using Ensemble Classifier," *Proceedings of the 2021 Fourth International Conference on Electrical, Computer and Communication Technologies*, September 2021.

Singer, Jonathan B., Terri A. Erbacher, and Perri Rosen, "School-Based Suicide Prevention: A Framework for Evidence-Based Practice," *School Mental Health*, Vol. 11, No. 1, 2019.

Singer, Natasha, "New A.I. Chatbot Tutors Could Upend Student Learning," *New York Times*, June 8, 2023.

Steiner, Elizabeth D., Sy Doan, Ashley Woo, Allyson D. Gittens, Rebecca Ann Lawrence, Lisa Berdie, Rebecca L. Wolfe, Lucas Greer, and Heather L. Schwartz, *Restoring Teacher and Principal Well-Being Is an Essential Step for Rebuilding Schools: Findings from the State of the American Teacher and State of the American Principal Surveys*, RAND Corporation, RR-A1108-1, 2022. As of October 12, 2023: https://www.rand.org/pubs/research_reports/RRA1108-4.html

Sumner, Steven A., Brock Ferguson, Brian Bason, Jacob Dink, Ellen Yard, Marci Hertz, Brandon Hilkert, Kristin Holland, Melissa Mercado-Crespo, and Shichao Tang, "Association of Online Risk Factors with Subsequent Youth Suicide-Related Behaviors in the U.S.," *JAMA Network Open*, Vol. 4, No. 9, 2021.

Treisman, Rachel, "13-Year-Old Boy with Autism Disorder Shot by Salt Lake City Police," NPR, September 9, 2020.

U.S. Department of Education, "What Is an Education Record?" webpage, undated. As of October 12, 2023:
https://studentprivacy.ed.gov/faq/what-education-record

U.S. Department of Education, "Family Educational Rights and Privacy Act (FERPA)," webpage, last updated August 25, 2021. As of October 12, 2023:
https://www2.ed.gov/policy/gen/guid/fpco/ferpa/index.html

U.S. Department of Education, *Artificial Intelligence and the Future of Teaching and Learning: Insights and Recommendations*, 2023.

U.S. Department of Health and Human Services, "Health Information Privacy," webpage, undated. As of October 12, 2023:
https://www.hhs.gov/hipaa/index.html

U.S. Department of Health and Human Services, "HHS Awards Funding to States, Tribes, and College Campuses to Help Prevent Youth Suicide, Part of the Biden-Harris Commitment to Addressing the Mental Health Crisis," press release, June 1, 2023.

U.S. Surgeon General, *Social Media and Youth Mental Health: The U.S. Surgeon General's Advisory*, 2023.

van Velzen, Laura S., Yara J. Toenders, Aina Avila-Parcet, Richard Dinga, Jill A. Rabinowitz, Adrián I. Campos, Neda Jahanshad, Miguel E. Rentería, and Lianne Schmaal, "Classification of Suicidal Thoughts and Behaviour in Children: Results from Penalised Logistic Regression Analyses in the Adolescent Brain Cognitive Development Study," *British Journal of Psychiatry*, Vol. 220, No. 4, April 2022.

van Vuuren, C. L., K. van Mens, D. de Beurs, J. Lokkerbol, M. F. van der Wal, P. Cuijpers, and M. J. M. Chinapaw, "Comparing Machine Learning to a Rule-Based Approach for Predicting Suicidal Behavior Among Adolescents: Results from a Longitudinal Population-Based Survey," *Journal of Affective Disorders*, Vol. 295, December 2021.

Vice News, "'They're Watching Us': Inside the Company Surveilling Millions of Students," video, December 13, 2022. As of October 12, 2023:
https://www.youtube.com/watch?v=o3YLpTWcclo

Vogels, Emily A., "Digital Divide Persists Even as Americans with Lower Incomes Make Gains in Tech Adoption," Pew Research Center, June 22, 2021.

Walsh, Colin G., Beenish Chaudhry, Prerna Dua, Kenneth W. Goodman, Bonnie Kaplan, Ramakanth Kavuluru, Anthony Solomonides, and Vignesh Subbian, "Stigma, Biomarkers, and Algorithmic Bias: Recommendations for Precision Behavioral Health with Artificial Intelligence," *JAMIA Open*, Vol. 3, No. 1, April 2020.

White House, *Blueprint for an AI Bill of Rights: Making Automated Systems Work for the American People*, 2022.

Wilcox, Holly C., Sheppard G. Kellam, C. Hendricks Brown, Jeanne M. Poduska, Nicholas S. Ialongo, Wei Wang, and James C. Anthony, "The Impact of Two Universal Randomized First- and Second-Grade Classroom Interventions on Young Adult Suicide Ideation and Attempts," *Drug and Alcohol Dependence*, Vol. 95, June 2008.

Woo, Ashley, Sabrina Lee, Andrea Prado Tuma, Julia H. Kaufman, Rebecca Ann Lawrence, and Nastassia Reed, *Walking on Eggshells—Teachers' Responses to Classroom Limitations on Race- or Gender-Related Topics: Findings from the 2022 American Instructional Resources Survey*, RAND Corporation, 2023. As of October 12, 2023:
https://www.rand.org/pubs/research_reports/RRA134-16.html

Zhang, Lei, Yuanxiao Fan, Jingwen Jiang, Yuchen Li, and Wei Zhang, "Adolescent Depression Detection Model Based on Multimodal Data of Interview Audio and Text," *International Journal of Neural Systems*, Vol. 32, No. 11, November 2022.

Zheng, Yufeng, Brian D. Christman, Matthew C. Morris, William B. Hillegass, Yunxi Zhang, Kimberly D. Douglas, Chris Kelly, and Lei Zhang, "Adolescent Behavioral Risk Analysis and Prediction Using Machine Learning: A Foundation for Precision Suicide Prevention," *Proceedings of SPIE Defense + Commercial Sensing*, May 2022.